Easy Origami

Easy Origami

Or`igami

A Colorful Introduction to Practical Paper Folding

Kazuo Kobayashi
Chiharu Sunayama

LARK
BOOKS

Editor: Jane LaFerla

Art Director: Dana Irwin

Production: Dana Irwin, Hannes Charen

Editorial Assistant: Evans Carter

Translation from the Japanese: Masako Miyagowa

Library of Congress Cataloging-in-Publication Data
Available

1 0 9 8 7 6 5 4 3 2 1

Published by Lark Books
50 College St.
Asheville, NC 28801, US

This book was originally published in Japanese by Nihon Vogue Co., Ltd. in 1996.

Copyright 1996 T. Seto

English translation 1998, Lark Books

Distributed by Random House,Inc.,in the United States, Canada, the United Kingdom, Europe,and
Asia
Distributed in Australia by Capricorn Link (Australia) Pty Ltd., P.O. Box 6651, Baulkham Hills Business
Centre, NSW 2153, Australia
Distributed in New Zealand by Tandem Press Ltd., 2 Rugby Rd., Birkenhead, Auckland, New Zealand

Printed in the United States

C o n t e n t s

Origami Magic

What is the enduring appeal of origami? In one word–magic! After all, few people can resist making something out of virtually nothing. Starting with a few sheets of paper and only using your hands for tools, you can create an array of intriguing objects by combining a few simple folds. With papers of different colors, sizes, and textures you can make infinite varieties of the same item, each with a unique look.

While folding paper into decorative shapes is almost as old as paper itself, the art form of origami grew and flourished in the Japanese culture. No one can say for certain how Japanese paper folding began but some scholars think it grew out of the precise folding patterns prescribed for making kimonos.

When a Buddhist monk brought paper making to Japan from China in the sixth century, paper was initially a precious commodity. Its cost limited its use for anything other than ceremonial purposes. Ceremonial origami followed rigid folding methods and learning it was more of a discipline than an artistic expression. Eventually paper became affordable to the common man, ceremonies changed, and origami achieved a popular following.

The spread of popular origami may have its roots in a Japanese tradition of wrapping gifts in white paper to signify that the recipient enjoys good luck. This custom was abbreviated to attaching a "noshi," a simple folded piece of white paper, to a gift. Making the noshi was the job of the housewife who was also responsible for making the kimonos for the family. Combining skills from these two duties may have naturally led to the practice of folding playthings from paper to amuse and occupy the children of the household.

PRACTICAL ORIGAMI

The projects in this book are colorful, fun to make, and practical. You can use them to make everyday table settings, holiday and party decorations, picnic and hiking accessories, gift wrapping, and items for gift giving. Whatever project you choose to make, you'll find folding with a purpose is an enjoyable way to learn about origami if you're a beginner or a great way to expand your knowledge if you're more experienced.

PAPER

You'll use a variety of papers as you work through the individual projects. You can purchase traditional origami paper in craft- or art-supply shops. This paper has one colored side and one white side. As necessary, project directions will instruct you where to place the

right and wrong sides of the paper before you begin folding.

Some projects instruct you to glue two sheets of paper together before folding, giving you a single sheet with two colored sides. Use white craft glue, applying a thin layer as evenly as possible to avoid making any lumps between layers. You may also use rubber cement or a solid glue stick. Make sure the glue is dry before you begin folding. Depending on the project, you may also need to use glue after you fold to hold edges together, secure a corner, or to fix a design element to another piece of the project.

Experimenting with papers is encouraged! With so many wonderful handmade papers available today, you have an unlimited "palette" to choose from. Gift-wrap paper, decorative foils, and even recycled newspapers and magazines can be used to give your projects a designer look. Just be mindful of using the weight of paper called for in the project if provided. You will not get the same results using lightweight paper if the instructions call for use of heavyweight.

Basics

On pages 50-54 you will find a section on folding basics. Included are a key to the symbols you will find in the project instructions, basic folding methods, and basic folds. Some projects will tell you to begin with a basic fold, such as Square-Fold B, before proceeding with Step 1 of that project. Refer to your basics section, complete

that fold, and you're ready to begin.

The projects in each chapter are arranged according to skill level with the easiest ones placed at the beginning of the section. If you're just starting out, try the easy ones first. You may want to make a few practice items before attempting the finished product.

When you're ready to fold and turn to the project illustrations, always read the general instructions first. You may occasionally spend time puzzling over a step. If you need help, refer to the basics section Don't get discouraged. It may take a few attempts to understand a fold. But once you finally "get-it," you've automatically expanded your knowledge and can apply it to other projects.

Precision will bring you the greatest success. Take time to line up edges, center folds as illustrated, and crease well when instructed. In origami each successive fold builds on the ones that come before it. Be precise, starting with the first fold, and you'll achieve the best results.

 # Plate Decorations

Quick sandwich meals and snacks don't have to be boring. Add interest to the ordinary when you serve them on top of these plate decorations. Use them at picnics on top of rattan plates for a disposable paper plate with panache, or lay them on a place mat for a quick and stylish serving solution when a regular plate is too much and a paper plate too plain. They're perfect for quick meals-on-the run. Instructions for projects 1-3 are on page 55.

Cloth Napkins

It's easy to add some interest to your table when you decorate with folded napkins. Create a bird, boat, house, and flower as additions to your place settings. Your guests or family won't be able to resist bread served in a napkin "basket." Not only will it look tantalizing, the bread will stay warm for serving. Instructions for projects 1-5 are on pages 56-57.

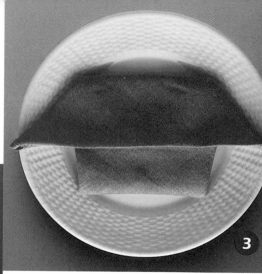

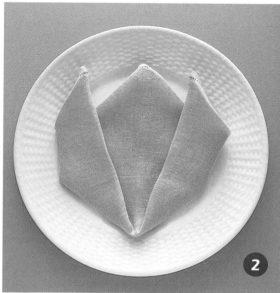

1

Fanciful-Fun Paper Napkins

Create instant fun for special occasions with these whimsical and entertaining designs made from printed-paper napkins. As a matter of fact, why wait! Turn an everyday family meal into a dinner to remember. Honor the men in your life with the easy-to-fold plaid shirt or bow tie. Use the same designs with floral-motif napkins to please the feminine gender. And kids will love the turtle or fox design. Instructions for projects 1-7 are on pages 58-60.

2

3

5

6

4

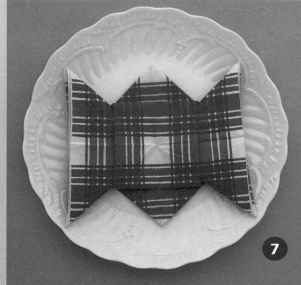

7

Kimono Napkins

Make these charming kimono miniatures

to grace your next oriental meal. They 'll become immediate conversation pieces. Use cloth napkins in a Japanese print for

an authentic touch, or make smaller versions out of paper to use as favors for the table. For a unique gift, make these out of handkerchiefs. After folding, place in a box and you have a clever treasure to give away.

Instructions for projects 1-3 are on pages 61-62.

Beasts of Burden

Invite a dragon to dinner (also a pig, rat, rabbit, and tiger). They won't eat much (or your guests) and they'll spend all evening delighting your human companions. Shown here as chopstick rests, you can also use them as knife rests. Follow the same directions using larger paper, place the animals on a place card, and you have instant souvenirs to give your guests as a reminder of one "wild" evening. Instructions for projects 1-5 are on pages 62-65.

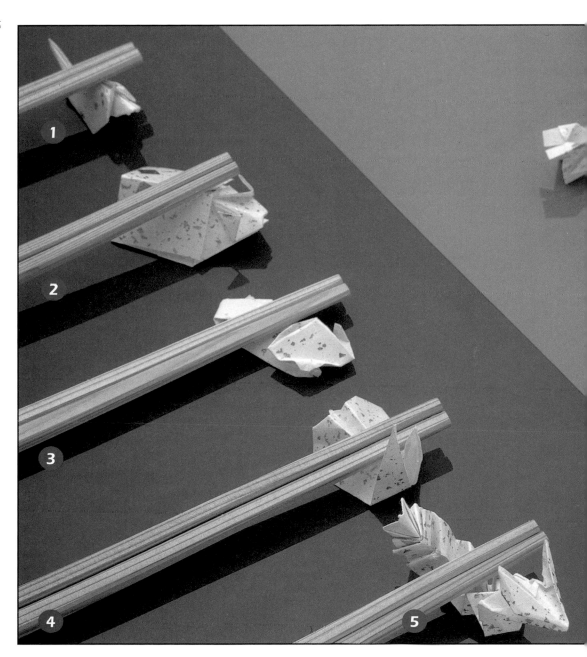

PARTY &
PICNIC

Picnics and Hiking

Who wants to be burdened with lots of stuff when you're set on a carefree day outdoors? With a few folds, a plastic cloth becomes a picnic basket that you can unfold at your destination and use as a tablecloth or ground cover. When you're hiking and don't want to carry bulky items, take a few sheets of foil and a few magazine pages along to make disposable cups and bowls. You can even make a waste basket from sheets of newspaper for holding your trash until you can throw it away. Instructions for projects 1-4 are on pages 66-68.

4

Wedding and Baby Showers

Use paper lace doilies to add a feminine touch to party items that are perfect for celebrating a marriage engagement, wedding, or birth. The individual candy dishes will brighten your table setting, and the wrappers can be made in any size to accommodate special party favors. Instructions for projects 1-2 are on page 66.

▼ Children's Party

Choose brightly colored paper for these children's party accessories. They're easy to make and will instantly tell your young guests that fun is the order of the day. For the candy bowls, use different sizes and colors of plain and patterned wrapping paper to add variety. For a unified look, choose paper that coordinates with the party's theme. Instructions for projects 1-4 are on pages 73-74.

Summertime Social

Set the mood for old-fashioned fun when you decorate your table for a summertime ice-cream social with these miniature parasols. Use lace doilies for a light, airy, romantic look. Then use brightly colored paper for the smaller mini parasols to add a lively touch.

Instructions for projects 1-3 are on page 75.

Brunch Coasters

Bring the bright feeling of Sunday morning to your table with these crisp floral coasters. They're the perfect highlight to a late and leisurely brunch. Each different design has its own special fold that you repeat and layer to create the pattern. Instructions for projects 1-4 are on page 76.

Hats

Remember making newspaper hats on a rainy day? Your imagination, and the right hat, helped you transform yourself into a hero or villain with a few easy folds. Recapture the fun of making your own for no other reason than just because. Or show a new generation how simple it is to create an afternoon of imaginative fun from almost nothing. Instructions for projects 1-4 are on pages 77-78.

Airplanes

Have a race, send a message, catch a breeze, or just see how far you can soar with these paper airplanes. Use pages from old magazines for recycled fun. Once you get started, experiment with your own designs to test your working knowledge of aerodynamics. Instructions for projects 1-4 are on pages 79-80.

Frames

Make receiving snapshots a spe-cial occasion for your friends and family. Rather than just tossing pictures in an envelope, create these colorful frames. With just a little extra effort you can highlight the good times, scenic wonders, happy smiles, and adoring glances that will brighten someone's day. Instructions for this project are on pages 80-81.

Handkerchief Surprises

Tired of giving friends the same old standard gifts? Try something different! Fold well-starched cloth bandannas or handkerchiefs into a floral-inspired design or a

2

gliding crane. For a change, use napkins instead of handkerchiefs for a hostess gift. Get a transparent corsage box from your florist to hold the "flower" and you'll have a unique surprise for a friend. Instructions for projects 1-2 are on pages 81-82.

1

Create your own storybook! Younger children will love having a book made just for them; older ones will enjoy making their own. You can also create mini-albums for holding snapshots, or make several books in the larger size so you can have a notebook for every occasion. For a bookmark that's hard to miss, make the easy-to-fold pencil. Instructions for projects 1-2 are on page 83.

Romantic Reminders

Recall the romance of bygone days when you use lacy paper doilies for these projects. Make a lace and ribbon envelope to hold a secret love letter. Deliver an unmistakable message to someone special by sending them a tiny valentine carried in the beak of a bird. State your romantic intentions in a small note and tuck it into the wings of an airy messenger who'll bring it to the one you love. Instructions for projects 1-3 are on pages 84-85.

Lucky Cranes

Fold these cranes for good luck! Use them to decorate your home, to make a mobile or garland by stringing them together, as table decorations, or to create a card that sends a message of best wishes. Whatever you choose to do, these cranes will remind you to celebrate the good fortune in your life. Instructions for projects 1-2 are on pages 85-87.

Book Covers and Bookmarks

Protect your books and at the same time have some folding fun. All avid readers will appreciate these book covers and bookmarks. Make them for yourself or give them as gifts. Use the covers as a unique way to gift wrap a book. Select the book, cover it, slip the book mark inside or use it as a gift tag. Instructions for projects 1-4 are on pages 88-90.

 Japanese Designs

Explore Japanese design when you make these small items. Being both beautiful and practical, they reflect the essence of Japanese craftsmanship. The accessories include a sewing kit, coin purse, coasters, and a variety of containers. Choose paper with Japanese prints to immediately capture the spirit of oriental decoration. Instructions for projects 1-7 are on pages 91-94.

BOXES & CONTAINERS

 Drawer Dividers

Get organized! With a few quick folds, you can have drawer dividers that are simple to make, inexpensive, and indispensable for taming clutter. Make the dividers in a variety of sizes to hold stationery, pencils, pens, and even paper clips. Use heavy paper, and for brightening your day, choose cheerful colors. Instructions for this project are on page 97.

 # Recycle It!

With a few sheets of old newspapers

you can make simple containers that will take care of dozens of uses. Why limit yourself to thinking they're just for scrap? Use them around the house to hold hobby or shop supplies. Put them in the kids' rooms to help them keep track of small game or puzzle pieces. Or use them around the house to organize special projects. If you want to use them to hold snacks as shown, make sure the food you put in them is individually wrapped or has a shell (like the peanuts). This will way you'll avoid getting ink on your edibles. Instructions for this project are on page 96.

Recycled Paper Vase and Dust Pan

Recycling not only makes sense, it can also be attractive. Don't let the old year just slip away. Recycle calendar pages into useful containers. Use them as waste baskets or as unusual vases for silk- or dried-flower arrangements. Choose a calendar page with a meaningful date and use it to make a memento for someone special. You can also quickly convert old newspapers to make convenient disposable dust pans. Instructions for projects 1-2 are on page 102-103.

Marbleized Gift Boxes

It's all in the presentation. . . If you don't have the size box you need for a special gift, make one! The person who is lucky enough to receive a surprise in a hand-folded box may have a hard time deciding which one is the real gift. Marbleized paper gives these boxes added interest. Learn the basic techniques, then alter the sizes to suit your needs. Instructions for projects 1-2 are on page 97.

Gift-Wrap Boxes

Eliminate the need for rolls of wrapping paper, spools of coordinating ribbon, sticky tape, and scissors. Make these boxes out of heavyweight gift-wrap paper and you'll instantly have decorative gift boxes without all the fuss and mess. Make your own paper ribbon and bows for added interest.

Instructions for projects 1-2 are on pages 99-100.

Candy Box

You can duplicate the look of an oriental lacquered box by choosing the right papers for this project. The dividers are individually folded inner boxes that line the bottom of the outer box, making it an ideal choice for giving gifts of food. The inner boxes not only protect the decorative outer box, but also provide separate compartments for grouping a variety of items. Instructions for this project are on pages 100-101.

Swan Container

An elegant folded swan can be both a unique presentation box for a gift as well as a treasured container to keep. When using as a gift box, cover the object with a folded piece of tissue paper in a coordinating color or a paper lace doily. Instructions for this project are on pages 101-102.

Traveling Companions

Have you ever had a hard time keeping foreign currency organized while traveling?

Avoid confusion by folding a variety of custom-made wallets for holding the different sizes of bills you'll be

handling. Using the same basic idea, you can make convenient holders for just about all the important

papers needed for your trip including passport, tickets, museum passes, and tissues! Instructions for pro-

jects 1-3 are on pages 106-107.

Organizers

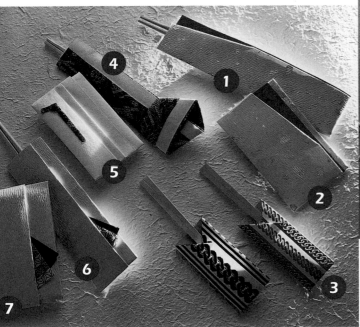

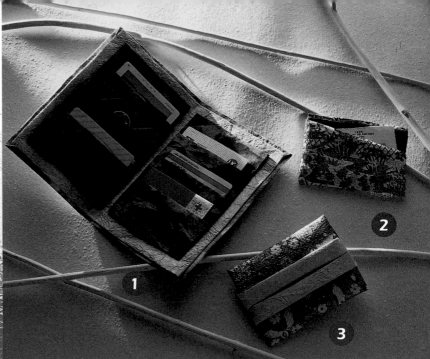

Card and Tissue Holders

You'll find a multitude of uses for these small containers. Aside from holding chopsticks, use the rectangular holders to keep your special artist brushes separate and clean; organize make-up items for purse or travel; or use them to hold a pocket comb. The smaller containers make handy organizers for gratuities when traveling or eating out. You can also use them as business card holders that are easy to tuck inside a pocket or briefcase. Instructions for projects 1-7 are on pages 103-105.

Look for authentic Japanese-made "washi" paper to make these items. You'll find it's lightweight, soft, and highly durable. These qualities make it the perfect material for creating handy pocket-sized containers for organizing small items. Once you learn to make your own, make extras to give as thoughtful gifts for friends and family. Instructions for projects 1-3 are on pages 107-109.

Guest-Bath Containers

Add instant color and charm to your guest bath with these containers that you can use for holding decorative soaps, bath oil beads, or wash cloths. The handled basket, "tulip-shaped" soap holders, and easy-to-fold box let you create a personal touch for all your overnight guests. Choose paper in bold prints that coordinate with your towels to make these small comforts hard to miss. Instructions for projects 1-3 are on pages 110-111.

 # Square Small-Item Containers

Keys, rings, necklaces, coins, earrings. . . Keep track of small items beautifully with

these colorful and attractive containers made especially to hold small items. Use patterned paper with

complementary solid colors to create infinite and exciting color combinations. Instructions for projects

1-3 are on pages 112-114.

Octagonal Small-Item Containers

These small containers are not only practical but eye-appealing. Explore the variations of this octagonal fold to make an endless array of containers to help you organize your life. But don't stop there–they make wonderful gift containers when you're giving something small and special.

Instructions for projects 1-5 are on pages 114-116.

 # Santa Napkins and Star Coasters

While children will love the Santa napkin holders, don't let the kids have all the fun! Create festive fun for your holiday get-togethers with these easy-to-fold favors that children of all ages can enjoy. Add star coasters made from metallic-colored paper to your table setting for extra sparkle. Instructions for projects 1-2 are on page 117.

Love Letters

You've written your innermost thoughts to the one you love. Your words are carefully chosen. Your handwriting is impeccable. Every expression has been crafted to delight the reader.

So. . . why settle for a plain envelope to take your heart away? Fall in love with these special valentine envelopes. They'll add the perfect grace note to your song of love. Instructions for projects 1-3 are on pages 118-119.

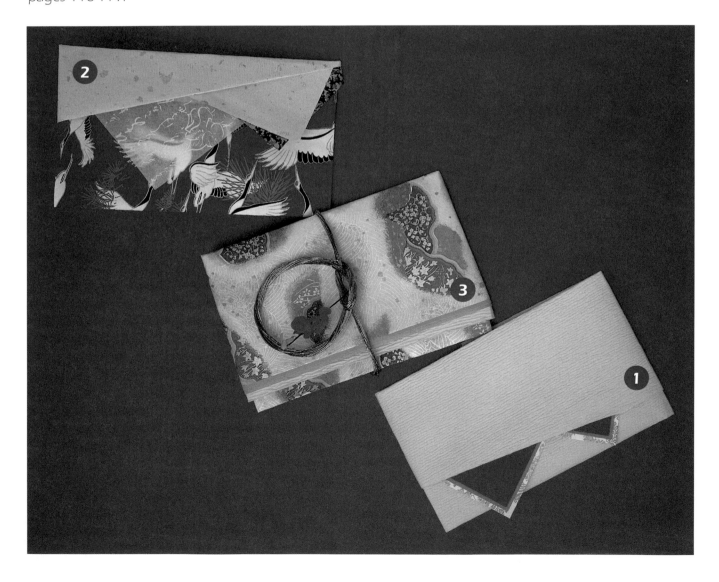

Valentine's Day

To show how much we care for someone on Valentine's Day, we often give more than our heart away. Make your own lovely gift wrap and containers to hold your heartfelt tokens of affection. If you want to let someone know how you feel without committing to an expensive card, send a simple handmade paper heart to declare your intentions. Instructions for projects 1-4 are on pages 119-121.

Holiday Season

Spread the holiday spirit to every room in the house. Add an old-fashioned, handmade touch to the season with these easy-to-make decorations. You'll soon have shiny stars, fancy coasters or cards, and a large bow for your door. Leave the shiny boot and stocking empty or fill them with fresh greenery, hang candy canes from their edges, or use them to hide small gifts to delight the children in your life. Instructions for projects 1-8 are on pages 122-125.

Wreath Greeting Card

Surprise everyone on your holiday mailing list when you send greetings featuring this hand-folded wreath. Involve the whole family with the cutting, folding, and assembling. You'll not only have unique cards to give, you'll have created an evening of family fun to treasure long after the holidays are over. Instructions for this project are on pages 126.

Folding Basics

Folding Key

The key to understanding the project illustrations lies in knowing these basics. Once you're familiar with them, you'll be able to follow the directions with ease. You'll see the same lines and symbols used in the individual projects. If you need help when working on the projects, refer back to these basics as needed. When you're totally comfortable with the basics and have completed some of the book's projects, experiment to create your own designs. You'll be surprised at the number of items you can make by knowing just a few simple folds.

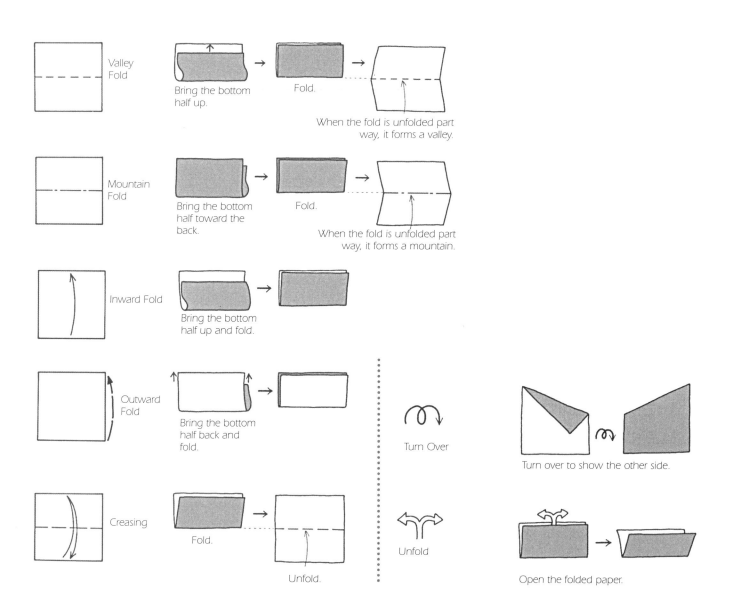

Valley Fold — Bring the bottom half up. Fold. When the fold is unfolded part way, it forms a valley.

Mountain Fold — Bring the bottom half toward the back. Fold. When the fold is unfolded part way, it forms a mountain.

Inward Fold — Bring the bottom half up and fold.

Outward Fold — Bring the bottom half back and fold.

Creasing — Fold. Unfold.

Turn Over — Turn over to show the other side.

Unfold — Open the folded paper.

Reverse Folding

Use these folds to make heads, beaks, etc.

INWARD REVERSE

1. Crease along the dotted line.
2. Push the tip open, fold, then flatten.
3. Reverse the fold at the crease line.

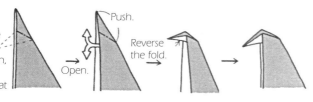

Push.

Open.

Reverse the fold.

OUTWARD REVERSE

!. Crease along the dotted line.
2. Unfold and push the tip back.
3. Reverse the fold at the crease line.
4. Fold again along the original crease, then flatten.

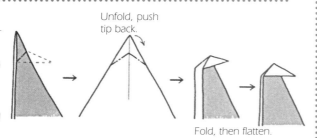

Unfold, push tip back.

Fold, then flatten.

Folding Methods

Folding in Half

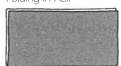

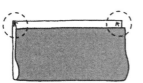

1. Bring the lower half over the upper half so the edges meet.

2. Hold the top center, crease the bottom center, then crease toward each end.

Folding a Triangle

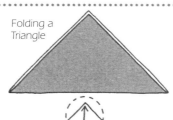

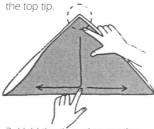

1. Bring the bottom tip to meet the top tip.

2. Hold the tip and crease the bottom edge.

Easy-to-fold Paper Sizes

Paper that is the size of your open hand is easy to handle. For the average adult that size is 6 x 6 inches (15 x 15 cm); for the average child, 5 x 5 inches (12.5 x 12.5 cm).

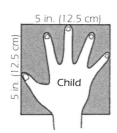

5 in. (12.5 cm)

5 in. (12.5 cm)

Child

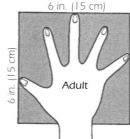

6 in. (15 cm)

6 in. (15 cm)

Adult

Folding While Holding

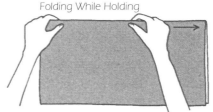

Hold the fold with the thumb and forefinger.

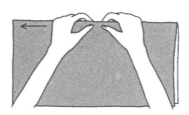

Slide your fingers to the center and move to both ends.

Folding on a flat surface.

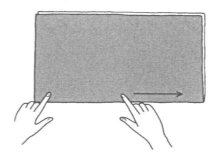

Press hard from the center toward both ends.

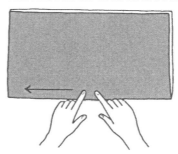

Basic Folds

These folds are used many times in origami to begin a project and are therefore called basic folds. Many of the project directions will tell you to begin with one of these basic folds before proceeding with Step 1 of that project. The individual directions will always give you the name of the fold and a page number in this section so you can refer to these directions for help if needed.

FOUR-CORNER FOLD

A. Corners To Center

1

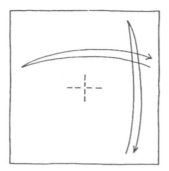

Fold the paper in half vertically and horizontally, making a cross-shaped crease at the center.

2

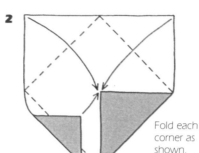

Bring the points of the four corners to the center of the cross.

Fold each corner as shown.

3

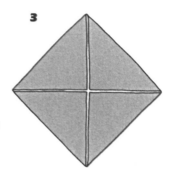

Crease well.

B. Double-Triangle Four-Corner Fold

1

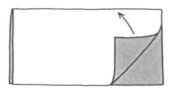

Fold paper in half so the wrong sides face out.

2

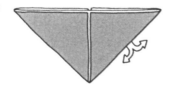

Bring the corners of the top flap to the fold line and crease well.

3

This completes half of this four-corner fold.

4

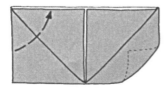

Fold both corners of the bottom flaps back, bringing them up to the fold line. Or, turn the paper over and repeat Step 2.

5

Open the edges on both sides.

6

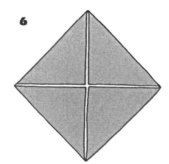

When open, crease the folds well.

A. This variation of the square fold is more suitable for larger pieces of paper that are lightweight and for soft-cloth projects such as napkin and handkerchief folding.

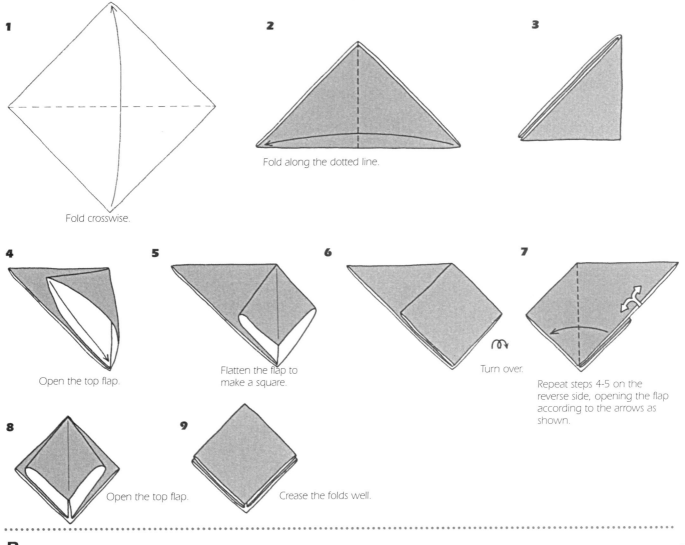

1

Fold crosswise.

2

Fold along the dotted line.

3

4

Open the top flap.

5

Flatten the flap to make a square.

6

Turn over.

7

Repeat steps 4-5 on the reverse side, opening the flap according to the arrows as shown.

8

Open the top flap.

9

Crease the folds well.

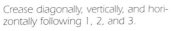

B. You may find this variation of the square fold to be more suitable for paper that is smaller or for paper of medium to heavyweight.

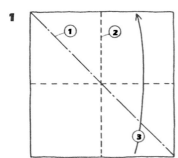

1

Crease diagonally, vertically, and horizontally following 1, 2, and 3.

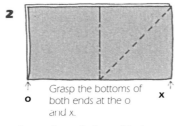

2

Grasp the bottoms of both ends at the o and x.

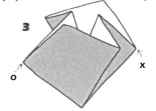

3

Push the o and x towards each other,

4

Crease the folds well.

TRIANGULAR FOLD

A. Folding a Square Before Making a Triangle

1

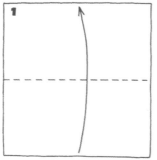

Fold in half along the dotted line.

2

Fold in half along the dotted line.

3

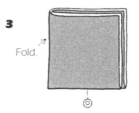

Fold.

This divides the square into fourths.

4

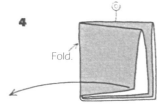

Fold.

Bring the right bottom corner of the upper flap to the left.

5

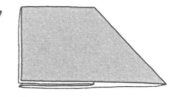

Fold the top down, making a triangle.

6

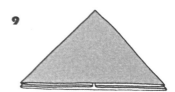

Fold and crease well.

7

Turn over.

8

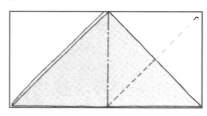

Bring the left bottom corner of the upper flap to the right following Step 4 and 5.

9

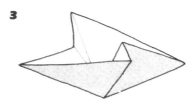

Fold and crease well.

B. Creasing Lines Before Making a Triangle.

1

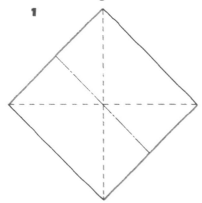

Crease along the dotted lines. Fold into a rectangle.

2

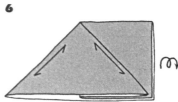

Hold the center while opening one end of the fold. Push the end toward the center.

3

Continue to push toward the center, reversing the fold along the crease lines.

4

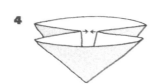

Repeat steps 2 and 3 on the other side.

5

Crease well.

Plate Decorations

Pages 8-9, Projects 1-3

1) Crane with Flapping Wings

Paper: You can use either a sheet with a printed side and a solid-color side, or a sheet of solid-color paper, size 8 x 12 inches (20.5 x 30.5 cm).

Instructions: At Step 2, the dotted line indicates a fold line that should be ⅓ the measurement of the large triangle.

2) Resting Crane

Paper: You can use either a sheet with a printed side and a solid-color side, or a sheet of solid-color paper, size 8 x 12 inches (20.5 x 30.5 cm).

Instructions: At Step 2, fold along the dotted line just slightly less than ⅓ of the large triangle.

3) Flying Crane

Paper: You can use either a sheet with a printed and a solid-color side, or a sheet of solid-color paper, size 8 x 12 inches (20.5 x 30.5 cm).

Instructions: At Step 2, the position of the dotted line determines the neck length.

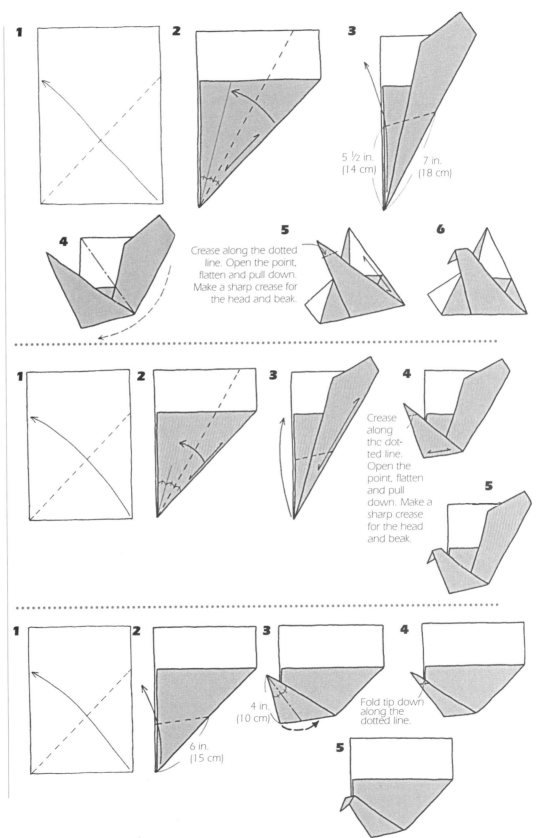

1 **2** **3** 5 ½ in. (14 cm) 7 in. (18 cm)

4 **5** Crease along the dotted line. Open the point, flatten and pull down. Make a sharp crease for the head and beak. **6**

1 **2** **3** **4** Crease along the dotted line. Open the point, flatten and pull down. Make a sharp crease for the head and beak. **5**

1 **2** 6 in. (15 cm) **3** 4 in. (10 cm) **4** Fold tip down along the dotted line. **5**

Cloth Napkins

Pages 10-11, Projects 1-5

1) Bird

Material: Cloth napkin, size 16 x 16 inches (40.5 x 40.5 cm).

Instructions: For best results, make "soft" folds rather than creasing each fold as you would do with paper. Begin with Four-Corner Fold A on page 52.

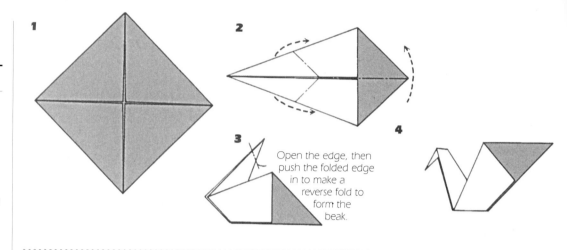

1

2

3

4

Open the edge, then push the folded edge in to make a reverse fold to form the beak.

3) House

Material: Cloth napkin, size 16 x 16 inches (40.5 x 40.5 cm).

Instructions: Begin with Four-Corner Fold A on Page 52. At Step 4, fold up on the dotted line and tuck the edge inside the roof.

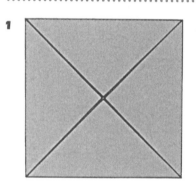

1

2

3

Fold the upper flaps along the dotted line.

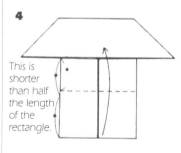

4

This is shorter than half the length of the rectangle.

5

Insert the flap under the roof.

2) Tulip

Material: Cloth napkin, size 16 x 16 inches (40.5 x 40.5 cm).

Instructions: At Step 2, bring both ends of the triangle up and fold the flap along the dotted lines. Begin with Four-Corner Fold A on page 52.

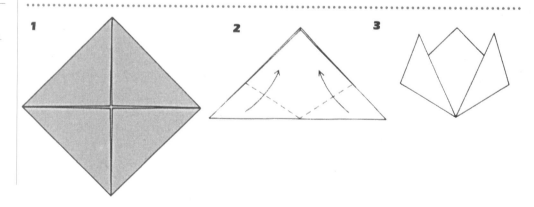

1

2

3

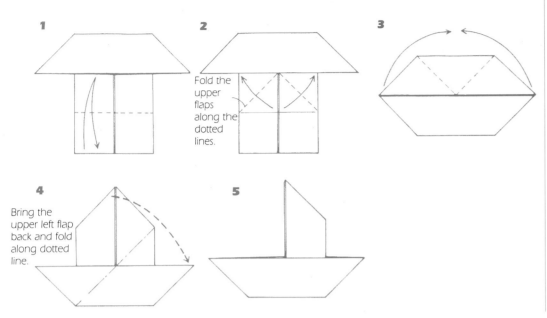

1

2
Fold the upper flaps along the dotted lines.

3

4) Boat

Material: Cloth napkin, size 16 x 16 inches (40.5 x 40.5 cm).

Instructions: Follow Steps 1-4 for project 3, the House. At Step 1 for this project, unfold along the dotted line rather than tucking the edge in as you did for project 3. Proceed with Steps 2-5. At Step 3, repeat the procedure with the lower flap, then bring both ends of the upper trapezoid up and fold the flaps along the dotted line.

5) Bread Basket

Material: Cloth napkin, size 22 x 22 inches (56 x 56 cm).

Instructions: At Step 1, fold the square into a rectangle as shown.

4
Bring the upper left flap back and fold along dotted line.

5

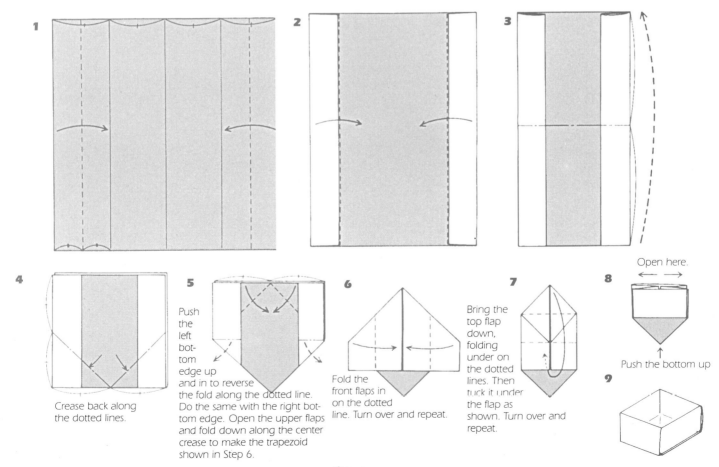

1

2

3

4
Crease back along the dotted lines.

5
Push the left bottom edge up and in to reverse the fold along the dotted line. Do the same with the right bottom edge. Open the upper flaps and fold down along the center crease to make the trapezoid shown in Step 6.

6
Fold the front flaps in on the dotted line. Turn over and repeat.

7
Bring the top flap down, folding under on the dotted lines. Then tuck it under the flap as shown. Turn over and repeat.

8
Open here.

Push the bottom up

9

Fanciful - Fun Paper Napkins

Pages 12-13, Projects 1-7

1) Fox

Paper: Printed paper napkin, size 12 x 12 inches (30.5 cm x 30.5 cm).

Instructions: At Step 2, the size of the fox's face is determined by the position of the backward fold.

Tip: If desired, use two dried beans for eyes, or draw them in with a black permanent marker.

2) Shirt

Paper: Printed paper napkin, size 12 x 12 inches (30.5 cm x 30.5 cm).

Tip: When choosing the paper, keep in mind that the color of the wrong side of the paper will become the color of the shirt collar.

3) Flower

Paper: Floral printed paper napkin, size 12 x 12 inches (30.5 cm x 30.5 cm).

Instructions: At Step 3, you can add variety to this design by changing the size of the triangles when you unfold them.

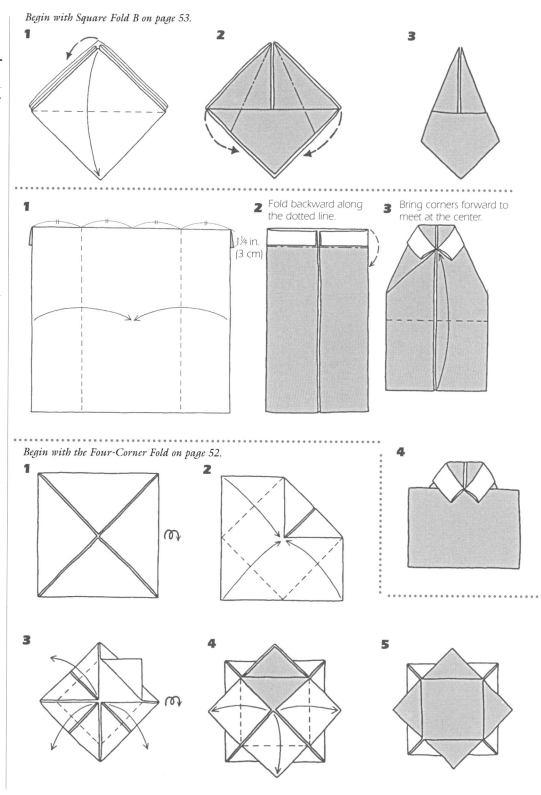

Begin with Square Fold B on page 53.

1   2   3

1

2 Fold backward along the dotted line.

1¼ in. (3 cm)

3 Bring corners forward to meet at the center.

Begin with the Four-Corner Fold on page 52.

1   2   4

3   4   5

1

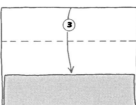

2

3

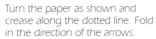

4) Pinwheel

Paper: Printed paper napkin, size 10 x 10 inches (25.5 cm x 25.5 cm).

Instructions: When measured from tip to tip, the size of the finished pinwheel should be the same size as the paper (see Step 6).

4

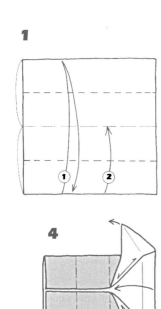

Holding the center of the paper with one hand, open the folds on the right of the paper slightly. Take the right edge of the paper and bring it to the center vertical line. Crease, then fold the two triangles up to the right. Repeat on the left side.

5

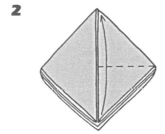

6

Turn the paper as shown and crease along the dotted line. Fold in the direction of the arrows.

Fold crosswise so the right side of the paper is showing.

1

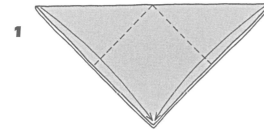

2

5) Turtle

In addition to paper you will need:
Scissors

Paper: Printed paper napkin, size 12 x 12 inches (30.5 cm x 30.5 cm).

Instructions: Follow Steps 1-7

3

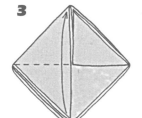

4

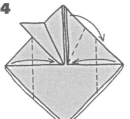

5

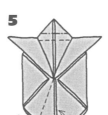

6

7

Cut the upper layer from the bottom point to the center. Then fold back on both sides along the dotted line.

7) Bow

Paper: Printed paper napkin, size 12 x 12 inches (30.5 cm x 30.5 cm).

Instructions: Begin with Triangular Fold A on page 54. At Step 12, press the innermost tip down to flatten the central square as shown in Step 13.

Begin with Triangular Fold A on page 54 then proceed from Step 1.

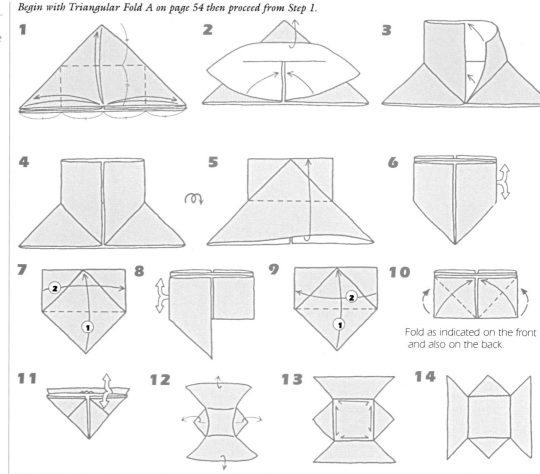

Fold as indicated on the front and also on the back.

6) Cicada

Paper: Printed paper napkin, size 12 x 12 inches (30.5 cm x 30.5 cm).

Instructions: To prepare the paper for Step 1, refer to project 5, the Turtle, on page 59. Follow Steps 1-2 of that project, then proceed from Step 1.

To begin, follow steps 1-2 of project 5, page 59. Then proceed with step 1.

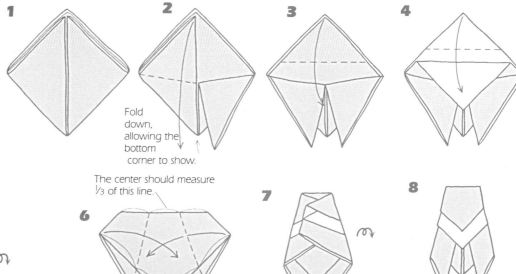

Fold down, allowing the bottom corner to show.

The center should measure 1/3 of this line.

Begin with Four-Corner Fold A on page 52 before proceeding to Step 1.

1

2

Turn over between each four-corner fold until reaching Step 5.

3

4

Turn over.

5

6

1 ¼ in. (3 cm)

¾ in. (2cm)

1

2

3

1 ¼ in. (3 cm)

4

5

11 in. (28 cm)

6

The vertical dotted lines determine the width of the kimono.

7

8

The horizontal lines determine the sleeve length.

9

Fold the bottom layer up two times.

Kimono Napkins

Page 14, Projects 1-3

1) Kimono with a "Face"

Material: Cloth or paper table napkin, size 14 x 14 inches (35.5 x 35.5 cm).

Instructions: Before starting Step 1, Begin with Four-Corner Fold A on page 52. At Step 5, choose one of the four squares to become the "face." The other squares will become the sleeves and bottom.

2) Kimono

Material: Cloth table napkin, size 14 x 35 inches (35.5 x 89 cm).

Instructions: The spaces between the bottom two dotted lines shown in Step 1 are the width of the collar. At Step 4, where you place the dotted line determines the length of the kimono.

3) Miniature Happi Coat

Material: Cloth or paper table napkin, size 14 x 14 inches (35.5 x 35.5 cm).

Instructions: The spaces between the top two dotted lines shown in Step 1 should be narrower than those you will fold in Step 3. These will become the collar.

Beasts of Burden
Chopstick/Knife Rests

Page 15, Projects 1-5,

1) Rat

Paper: Heavyweight white paper, size 2 ½ x 2 ½ inches (6.5 x 6.5 cm).

Instructions: At Step 2, unfold the upper flaps you made following Step 1. Open slightly and bring the top edges of each flap to the center line as shown in Step 2. At Step 3, fold the upper flaps to the left, then turn over. At Step 4, fold only the left-hand flaps on the dotted lines. At Step 6, fold the head first, then fold the tail accordingly to balance the head. To make the ears at Step 6, fold the upper left flap under, then tip out. At Step 7, open the flap, then reverse and flatten the fold on the dotted line.

Tip: You can make a larger version using a bigger square of paper.

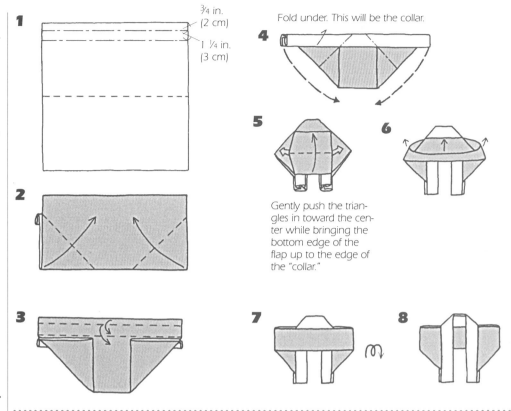

³⁄₄ in. (2 cm)
1 ¼ in. (3 cm)

4 — Fold under. This will be the collar.

5 — Gently push the triangles in toward the center while bringing the bottom edge of the flap up to the edge of the "collar."

6

7

8

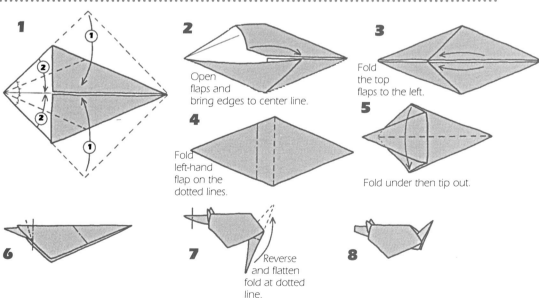

1

2 — Open flaps and bring edges to center line.

3 — Fold the top flaps to the left.

4 — Fold left-hand flap on the dotted lines.

5 — Fold under then tip out.

6

7 — Reverse and flatten fold at dotted line.

8

1

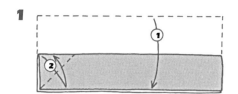

2

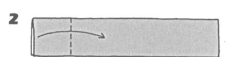

3

Open flap to make triangle shown in Step 4.

4

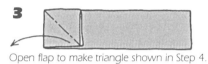

5

Crease along dotted line, then open.

6

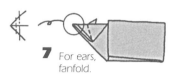

7 For ears, fanfold.

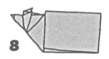

8

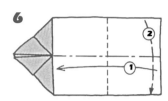

2) Pig

Paper: Heavyweight white paper, size 1 ½ x 4 inches (4 x 10 cm).

Instructions: At Step 3, open and move the fold to make the triangle shown in Step 4, At Step 5, crease well along the dotted line. Open the fold, moving and positioning the small upper square as shown in Step 6. Crease well. At Step 7, fanfold at the outer left tips to make the ears.

Tip: You can make a larger version using a bigger rectangle of paper.

3) Tiger

Paper: Heavyweight white paper, size 1 ½ x 2 ½ inches (4 x 6.5 cm).

Instructions: For the face and ears at Steps 3 and 4, make sharp folds by creasing well.

Tip: You can make a larger version using a bigger rectangle of paper.

1 **2** **3**

4

5 **6** **7** **8**

9

4) Rabbit

Paper: Heavyweight white paper, size 2 x 2 inches (5 x 5 cm).

Instructions: At Step 3, open the left flap, bring it up, then fold along the dotted lines while reversing the fold. Next, open the top fold, push it in, and fold along the dotted lines while reversing the fold. At Step 4, cut the left fold to make the ears.

Tip: You can make a larger version using a bigger square of paper.

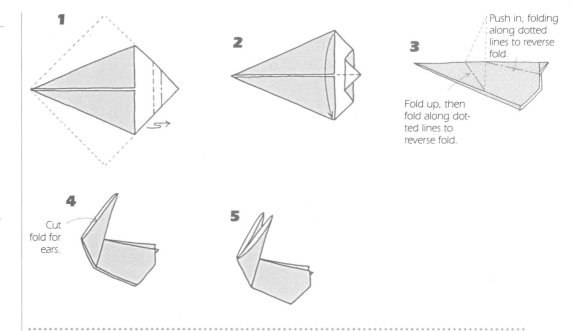

5) Dragon

Paper: Heavyweight white paper, size 1 ½ x 7 (or longer) inches (4 x 18 [or longer] cm).

Instructions: Steps 5-8 are an enlargement showing how to fold the tip after completing Stp 4. At Step 5-8, push up the bottom of the right triangle indicated by the dotted lines. Bring this triangle to the left and fold. Repeat on the other side. At Step 11, fanfold in small sections staritng from the top. At Step 15, crease well to sharpen the folds, then shape the tail by pulling gently out.

Tip: You can make a larger version using a bigger rectangle of paper.

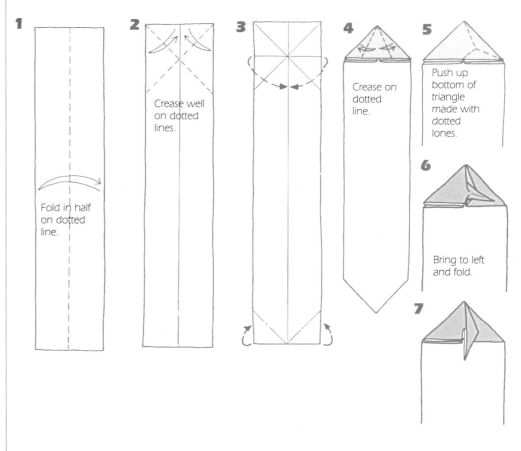

8

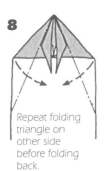

Repeat folding triangle on other side before folding back.

9

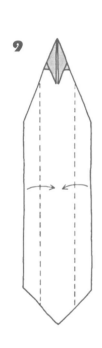

10

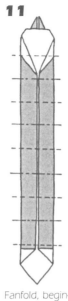

11

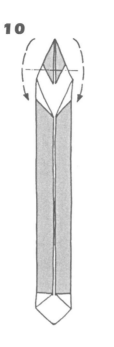

Fanfold, beginning at the top.

12

Fold entire piece in half.

13

I fold the body and bring the head up.

14

Tilt the body as shown in Step 15.

15

16

PARTY AND PICNIC

Wedding and Baby Showers

Page 18, Projects 1-2

1) Party Favors

In addition to paper you will need:
Ribbon or gift-wrap wire

Paper: Round paper doily, 12 inches (30.5 cm) in diameter. Gift-wrap paper, size 12 x 12 inches (30.5 x 30.5 cm).

Instructions: Place the doily on top of the paper with the right side of the gift-wrap paper facing out. Place your favor in the center and tie closed with the ribbon wire.

2) Candy Dishes

Paper: Round paper doily, 6 inches (15 cm) in diameter. Heavy paper, size 6 ½ x 6 ½ inches (17 x 17 cm).

Instructions: Before folding, place the paper doily on top of the sheet of heavy paper.

Picnic and Hiking

Pages 16-17, Projects 1-4

4) Picnic Basket

Material: Use a plastic table cloth or ground cover, size 72 x 72 inches (1.8 x 1.8 m).

Instructions: These instructions are for a square cloth. If you have a rectangular cloth, follow the instructions for project 1, the newspaper trash bin on page 67.

1

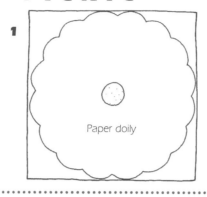

Paper doily

2

3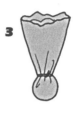

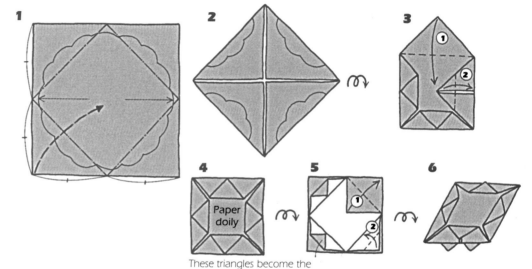

1

2

3
①
②

4

Paper doily

5
①
②

6

These triangles become the feet of the candy dish.

1

Ground cloth

2 Start here.

3

Follow Steps 3-13 for project 1 on page 67. When you've completed those steps, continue with Step 4.

4

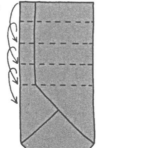

5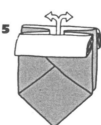

6

1

Place two sheets of paper on top of each other.

2

3

Crease well.

4

Open to make a triangle.

① Grip lower layers.

②

5

6

②

②

Crease well

①

③

Fold right half over left

Crease well

7

8

9

10

Crease well.

11

12 Fold the bottom layer under.

13

Crease along the dotted line.

14

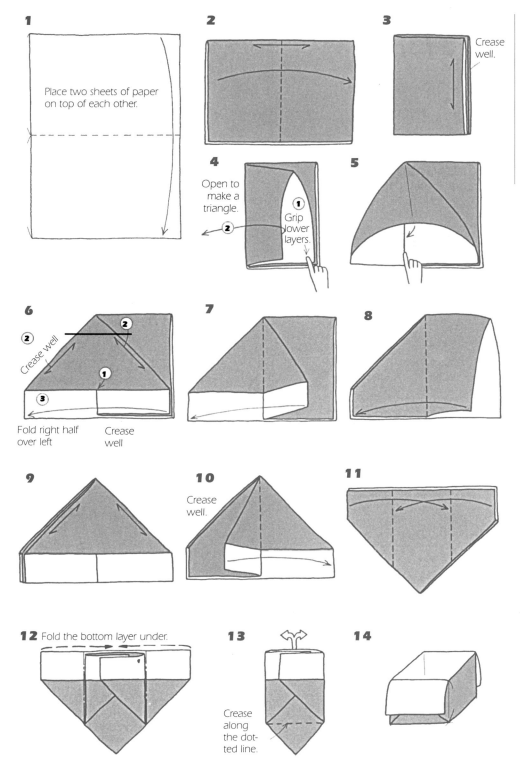

1) Newspaper Trash Bin

Paper: Two sheets of newspaper.

Tip: Place the sheets of newspaper on top of each other and fold as one. The finished size of the bin is determined by the placement of the folds in Step 11.

2) Aluminum Foil Cup

Material: Two sheets of aluminum foil, size 10 x 10 inches (25.5 x 25.5 cm).

Instructions: Place the sheets on top of each other with the shiny sides out.

Tip: When you use the cups, support them by holding them near the bottom.

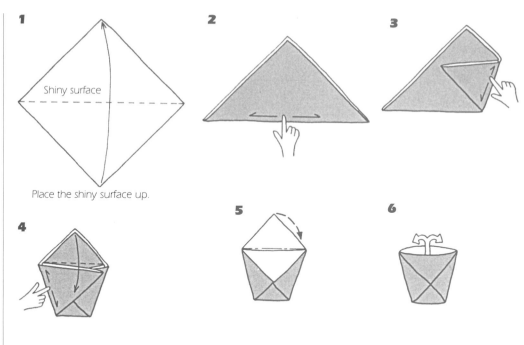

1

Shiny surface

Place the shiny surface up.

3) Bowls

Material: Pages from old magazines and aluminum foil, sizes approximately 8 x 8 inches (20.5 x 20.5 cm) each.

Instructions: Place the sheet of aluminum foil on top of the magazine page and fold as one.

Foil Bowls

Page 19

Paper: One sheet each of heavyweight paper and aluminum foil, both size 9 ½ x 14 inches (24 x 35.5 cm) for a larger bowl and 8 x 12 ½ inches (20.5 x 31.5 cm) for a smaller bowl.

Instructions: Begin by placing the papers on top of each other with the aluminum foil facing out as shown in Step 1. At Step 5, fold carefully to avoid tearing.

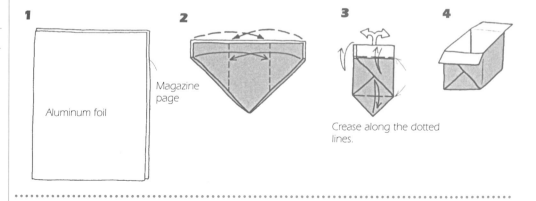

Crease along the dotted lines.

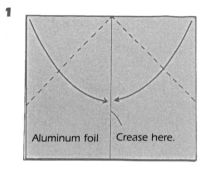

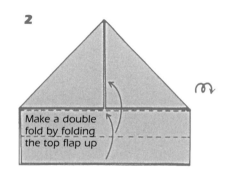

3

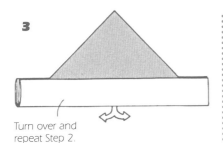

Turn over and repeat Step 2.

4

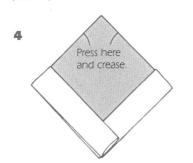

Press here and crease.

5

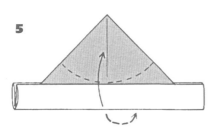

6

Begin with Square Fold B on page 52 to fold paper for Step 1 before proceeding with Steps 2-7.

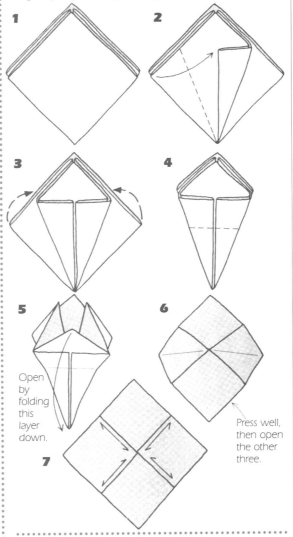

1

2

3

4

5 Open by folding this layer down.

6 Press well, then open the other three.

7

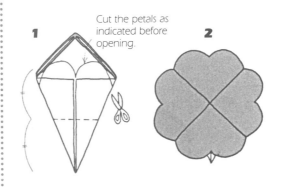

1 Cut the petals as indicated before opening.

2

Party Plates

Pages 20-21, Projects 1-6

For projects 1, 2, and 3 you'll be using this basic fold.

1) Eight-Petal Plate

In addition to paper, you will need:
Pencil
Scissors

Paper: White medium-weight paper, size 11 x 11 inches (28 x 28 cm).

Instructions: Follow Steps 1-7 of the basic fold for this project.

Tip: Draw the outline of the petals with a pencil before you cut.

2) Crimped-Edge Cake Plate

In addition to paper, you will need:
Crimping (pinking) shears

Paper: White medium-weight paper, size 10 x 10 inches (25.5 x 25.5 cm).

Instructions: Follow Steps 1-7 of the basic fold for this project.

Tip: After completing Step 4, cut the edges of the triangle with the shears.

1

Trim before opening.

2

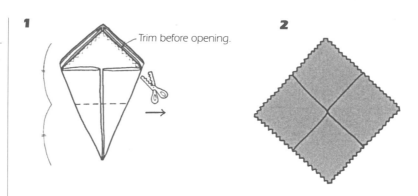

3) Round Plate

In addition to paper, you will need:

Scissors

Paper: Light lavender medium-weight paper, size 13 x 13 inches (33 x 33 cm) for a large plate; 10 x 10 inches (25.5 x 25.5 cm) for a small plate.

Instructions: Follow Steps 1-7 for the basic fold for this project.

Tip: After completing Step 4, cut in an arc.

Cut before unfolding.

1

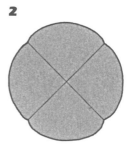

2

4) Leaf Plate

Paper: For the large leaf you can use mottled brown paper, shiny green for a tropical effect, or select a variety of fall colors, size 6 ½ x 6 ½ inches (16.5 x 16.5 cm). For the small leaf use rainbow-colored paper (or a color of your choice), size 4 x 4 inches (10 x 10 cm).

Tip: At Step 3, imagine a favorite leaf and fanfold accordingly to make its veins.

1

2

3

Fanfold to make the creases.

Start here.

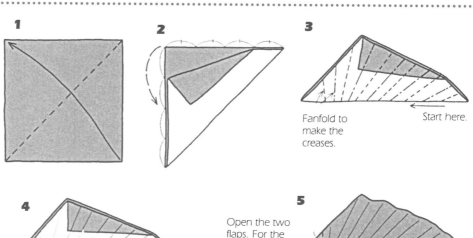

4

Fold with a slight curve along the dotted line.

5

Open the two flaps. For the large plate, fold under along the dotted line.

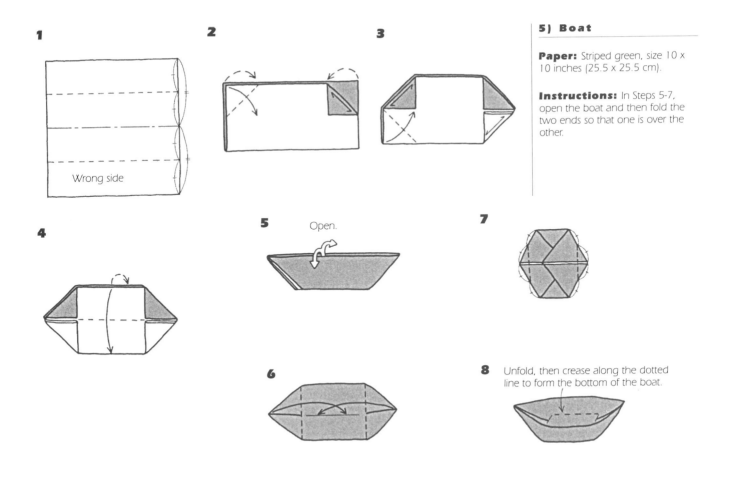

1

Wrong side

2

3

4

5 Open.

6

7

8 Unfold, then crease along the dotted line to form the bottom of the boat.

5) Boat

Paper: Striped green, size 10 x 10 inches (25.5 x 25.5 cm).

Instructions: In Steps 5-7, open the boat and then fold the two ends so that one is over the other.

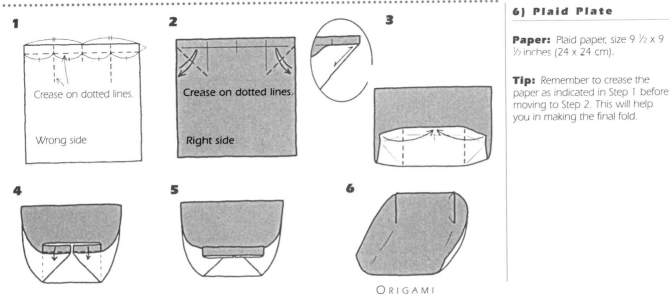

1

Crease on dotted lines.

Wrong side

2

Crease on dotted lines.

Right side

3

4

5

6

6) Plaid Plate

Paper: Plaid paper, size 9 ½ x 9 ½ inches (24 x 24 cm).

Tip: Remember to crease the paper as indicated in Step 1 before moving to Step 2. This will help you in making the final fold.

ORIGAMI

Party Coasters

Page 20, Projects 1-9

1) Basic Flower

In addition to paper you will need: White craft glue

Paper: Each coaster uses two sheets of paper, size 3 x 3 inches (7.5 x 7.5 cm).

Instructions: The different shapes for the coasters are determined by the basic folds and how you cut the paper for each design. For projects 00-00, begin with the Basic 10-Fold shown below. It divides the paper into 10 equal pie-shaped pieces. For projects 00-00 begin with the Basic 12-Fold shown below. It divides the paper into 12 equal pie-shaped pieces. Using the 10-Fold will give you a five-petal design; the 12 -fold will give you a six-petal design. Once you cut your shapes, unfold them and glue each on separate 3 x 3 inch (7.5 x 7.5 cm) papers.

Tip: Experiment with different colors and patterns of papers for almost endless varieties of these easy coasters.

(1) 1

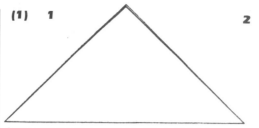

Begin with the Basic 10-Fold of Basic 12-Fold (shown here: Basic 10-Fold).

2

Cut to form petals.

Beginning with the Basic 10-Fold will give you five petals; beginning with the Basic 12-Fold gives you six.

2,7 Variations on the Basic 12-Fold

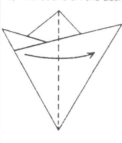 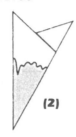 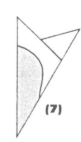

(2) **(7)**

3

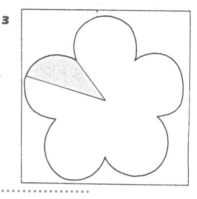

3,4,5,6,8,9 Variations on the Basic 10-Fold

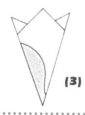 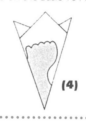 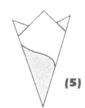 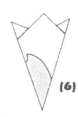 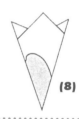 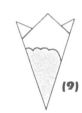

(3) **(4)** **(5)** **(6)** **(8)** **(9)**

Basic 10-fold

1

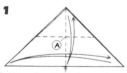

Fold and unfold along dotted lines to make point A.

2

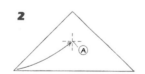

3

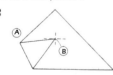

4

Fold a line connecting point B to the center crease, then unfold. Next, fold the bottom edge up along that line.

5

6

7

Basic 12-fold

1

Crease at center and at point A.

2

3

Crease at point B.

4

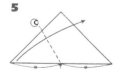

Fold and unfold.

5

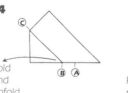

6

Fold on a line connecting point C made in Step 4 to the center crease.

7

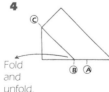

8

Children's Party

Page 21, Projects 1-4

1) Candy Bowls

Paper: Plain or patterned wrapping paper. For a large bowl, size 9 ½ x 9 ½ inches (24 x 24 cm). For a small bowl, size 8 x 8 (20 x 20 cm).

Instructions: Begin with the Four-Corner Fold on page 52 then follow steps 1-8. At Step 7 be sure to crease the folds well. At Step 8, unfold as shown while gently pushing out to shape the four corners of the bowl.

Tip: You can use one sheet of paper, or fold two together using one plain sheet and one patterned sheet. If you use two sheets, lay one sheet on top of the other with right sides facing out, then fold as one.

2) Animal-Face Toothpick Caps

In addition to paper you will need:
Scissors
Glue
Toothpicks

Paper: Plain paper in a variety of colors, size 3 x 3 inches (7.5 x 7.5 cm). Each animal is made from two sheets of different color papers. Place the two sheets on top of each other with the right sides facing out and fold as one.

Instructions: Follow Steps 1-8 to make the basic face. The different animal faces are determined by how you cut or fold the ears and the features you draw.

Tip: Make your first fold to the corner so the ear color faces out.

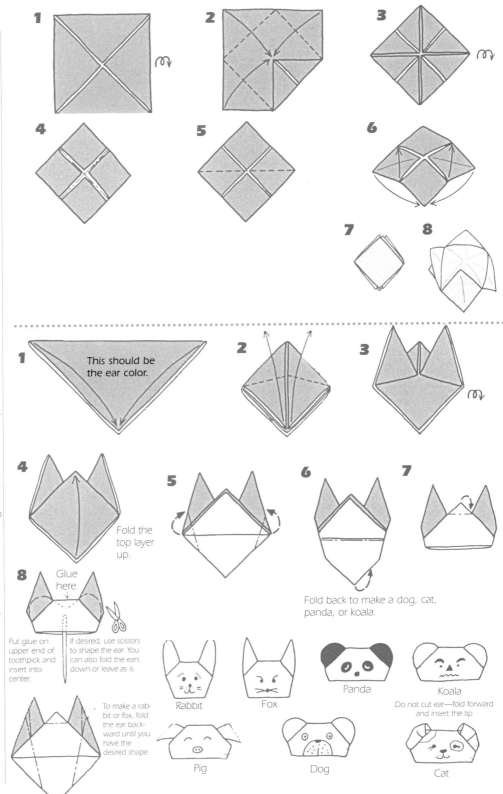

This should be the ear color.

Fold the top layer up.

Fold the top layer up.

Fold back to make a dog, cat, panda, or koala.

Glue here.

Put glue on upper end of toothpick and insert into center.

If desired, use scissors to shape the ear. You can also fold the ears down or leave as is.

To make a rabbit or fox, fold the ear backward until you have the desired shape.

Rabbit

Fox

Panda

Koala
Do not cut ear—fold forward and insert the tip

Pig

Dog

Cat

3) Toothpick Holder

In addition to paper you will need: Scissors

Paper: Heavy craft paper, size 10 ½ x 10 ½ inches (27 x 27 cm).

Instructions: First fold paper to make a triangle, then follow Steps 1-3.

Tip: Step 2 shows how to make a handle by cutting and folding. Make sure to fold the front layer forward and the back layer to the back.

1

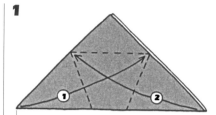

Bring this tip to the opposite side.

2

Cut as shown to make a handle ¾ inch (2 cm) wide. Fold the layers of the cut triangle down in the back and the front.

3

4) Napkin Ring

Paper: Two strips of paper of different colors, each size ⅜ inch (1 cm) wide by 26 inches (66 cm) long.

Instructions: Place the strips on top of each other with the right sides facing out. As you fold, weave over and under as shown.

Make the first fold at 6 ½-inches (16.5 cm) measured from the bottom of the strip.

1 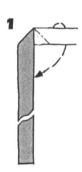 **2**  **3** 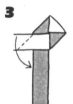 **4** 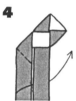 **5**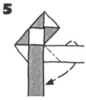

6

Repeat Steps 3-6

7

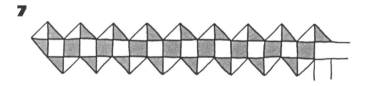

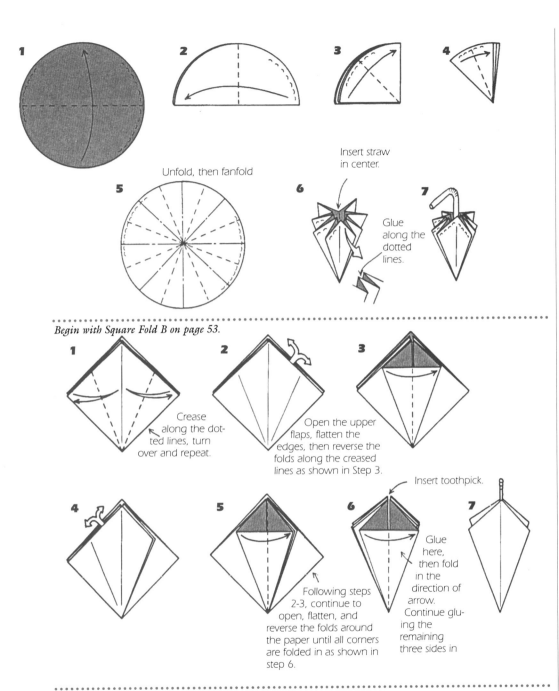

1

2

3

4

Unfold, then fanfold

5

6

Insert straw in center.

7

Glue along the dotted lines.

Begin with Square Fold B on page 53.

1

Crease along the dotted lines, turn over and repeat.

2

Open the upper flaps, flatten the edges, then reverse the folds along the creased lines as shown in Step 3.

3

4

5

Following steps 2-3, continue to open, flatten, and reverse the folds around the paper until all corners are folded in as shown in step 6.

6

Insert toothpick.

Glue here, then fold in the direction of arrow. Continue gluing the remaining three sides in

7

Follow Steps 1-5 for Project 2, before proceeding to Step 6 below.

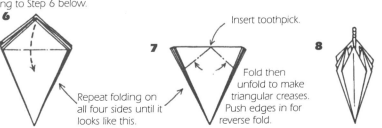

6

Repeat folding on all four sides until it looks like this.

7

Insert toothpick.

Fold then unfold to make triangular creases. Push edges in for reverse fold.

8

Summertime Social

Page 22, Projects 1-3

1) Lacy Parasol

In addition to paper you will need:
Plastic or paper "bendable" drinking straw
White craft glue

Paper: Lace doily, size 12 inches (30.5 cm) in diameter.

Instructions: Fold the paper as shown to make 16 pie-shaped creases. Unfold, then fanfold along the crease lines. Glue the fanfolds together as shown in Step 6, leaving enough space for the inserted straw.

2) Mini Parasol

In addition to paper you will need:
Toothpicks
White craft glue

Paper: Printed paper, size 3 x 3 inches (7.5 x 7.5 cm).

Instructions: Begin with Square Fold B on page 52. Crease the folds well then glue all four sides, leaving room for the inserted toothpick.

3) Miniature Parasol

In addition to paper you will need:
Toothpicks
White craft glue

Paper: 6 x 6 inches (15 x 15 cm).

Instructions: Begin with Square Fold B on page 53. Then follow Steps 1-5 for project 2 on page 75. At Step 6 for this project, fold the triangular flaps in and down. At Step 7, open the triangle and push the ends in to make a reverse fold, creasing well.

Brunch Coasters

Page 23, Projects 1-4

In addition to paper you will need:

White craft glue

Paper: Printed paper, size 3 x 3 inches (7.5 x 7.5 cm).

Instructions: For each design make the same fold for that design on five to seven sheets of paper referring to individual instructions. When folded, place the papers on top of each other, making sure that the point marked by the star in the illustrations is in the center. Arrange them to look like a flower. For help with placement, refer to the photo on page 23. Once in place, glue each layer together.

Tip: Using printed paper with a solid color on the reverse side will create the effect in the photo on page 23. Or, use two sheets for each fold using one printed and one solid-color sheet. Place the papers on top of each other with right sides facing out and fold as one.

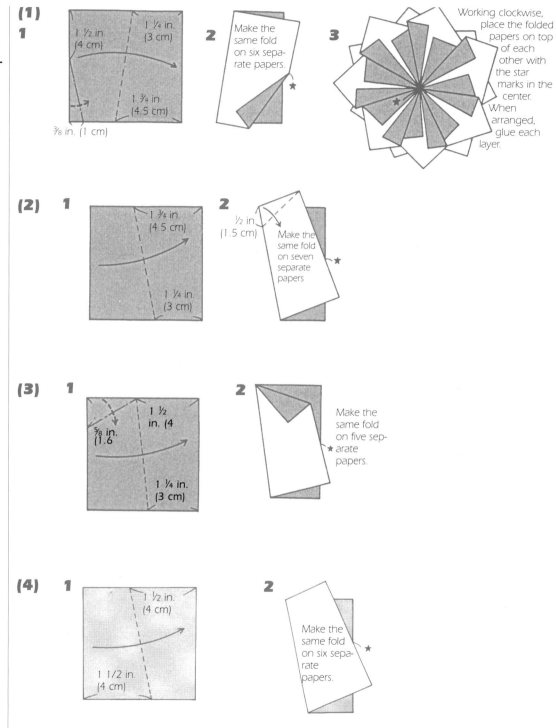

(1) 1 1 ½ in. (4 cm) — 1 ¼ in. (3 cm) — 1 ¾ in. (4.5 cm) — ⅜ in. (1 cm)

2 Make the same fold on six separate papers. ★

3 Working clockwise, place the folded papers on top of each other with the star marks in the center. When arranged, glue each layer.

(2) 1 1 ¾ in. (4.5 cm) — 1 ¼ in. (3 cm)

2 ½ in. (1.5 cm) Make the same fold on seven separate papers ★

(3) 1 1 ½ in. (4 — ⅝ in. (1.6 — 1 ¼ in. (3 cm)

2 Make the same fold on five separate papers. ★

(4) 1 1 ½ in. (4 cm) — 1 1/2 in. (4 cm)

2 Make the same fold on six separate papers. ★

1

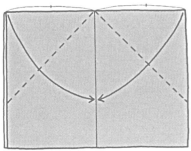

2

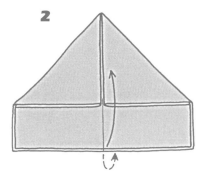

Newspaper Hats

Page 24, Projects 1-4

1) Triangle Hat

Paper: One sheet of newspaper.

Instructions: At Step 3, open the hat at the bottom. At step 5, adjust the height of your hat by changing the level of the dotted line.

3

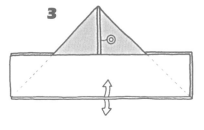

4

5

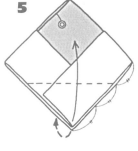

6

7

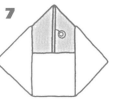

2) Brimmed Hat

In addition to paper you will need: White Craft Glue

Paper: Two sheets of newspaper.

Instructions: Place the two sheets on top of each other and fold as one, following the directions for Steps 1-4.

Tip: At Step 4 shape the brim anyway you want.

1

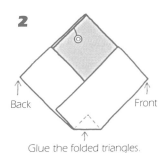

Fold in.

2

Back   Front

Glue the folded triangles.

3

Open the bottom and turn up to make the brim.

4

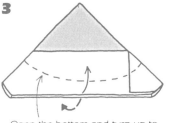

3) Rectangular Hat

Paper: One sheet of newspaper.

Instructions: Follow Steps 1-8.

Tip: When you're finished making the hat, gently squeeze the lower edge to open. Take care when putting on your hat so it won't tear.

Start by folding the sheet in half.

1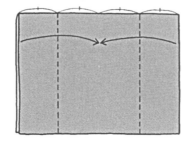

2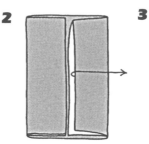

3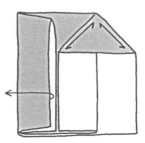

4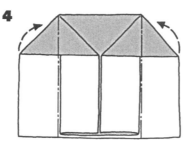

Fold the right and left flaps back.

5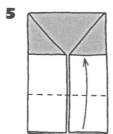

6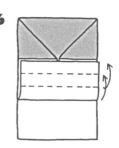

7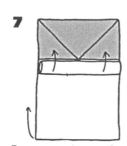

Turn over and repeat Step 6.

8

4) High-Crowned Hat

Paper: One sheet of newspaper.

Instructions: Cut the sheet into a square before folding. Begin by folding crosswise.

1

2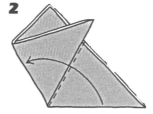

3

4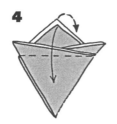

5

6

78   ORIGAMI

(1) 1

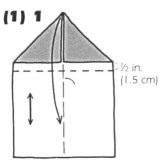

½ in.
(1.5 cm)

Crease along the vertical line and
fold along the horizontal dotted line.

2

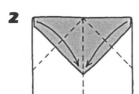

3

1 Fold in half.

2 Fold the flaps back
along the diagonal lines.

4

Paper: One magazine page for
each airplane.

Instructions: Follow the
instructions for your chosen design.

Tip: Be sure to crease well at
every step.

---

(2) 1

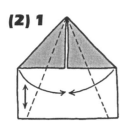

Cut paper into a square.

2

Fold
down.

3

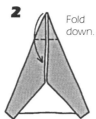

Turn over and fold in half.
Fold the flaps back along
the diagonal dotted lines.

4

How To Make a Plane that Flies Well

A paper airplane that is folded with the grain of the paper will fly
better than one that isn't. To determine which way to place the
paper before you begin folding, take a sample page from the
magazine you're using and tear as shown in the top figure.

If the paper tears smoothly, place the sheet you'll be using for
the airplane the same way before folding.

If the paper does not tear smoothly, as shown in the bottom
figure. turn the sheet you'll use for the airplane around. If you
imagine that the sheet has arrows showing you the way, you
would want them to point up and down rather that sideways.

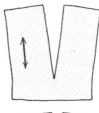

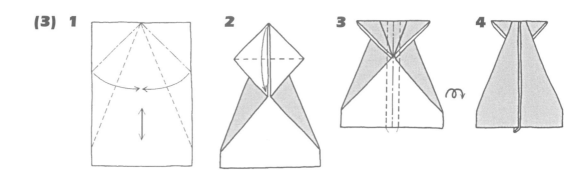

(3)

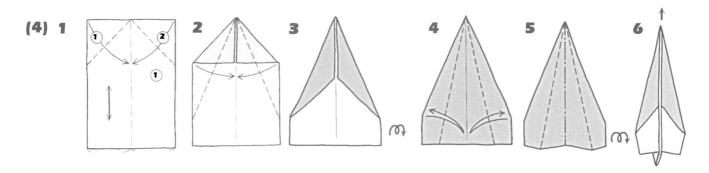

(4)

Frames

Page 26, Projects 1-2

1) Rectangular Frame

In addition to paper you will need:
Double-sided tape

Paper: Choose a medium-weight paper. The size you use depends on the size of the picture.

Instructions: Place your picture on the paper, determine your fold lines, trim the excess paper, and fold as shown. Make sure to double-fold the edges as shown in Step 2 to give the frame more body. Fold the top and bottom edge so they are $1/16$ of an inch (.2 cm) longer than the side edges.

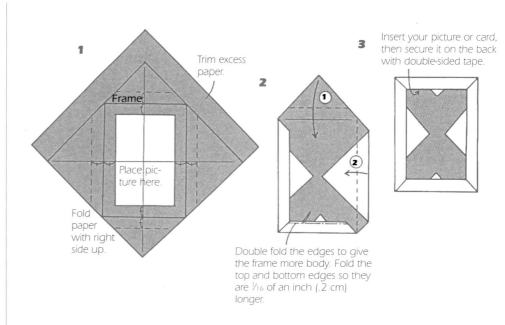

1 Frame Trim excess paper.

Place picture here.

Fold paper with right side up.

2

3 Insert your picture or card, then secure it on the back with double-sided tape.

Double fold the edges to give the frame more body. Fold the top and bottom edges so they are $1/16$ of an inch (.2 cm) longer.

1

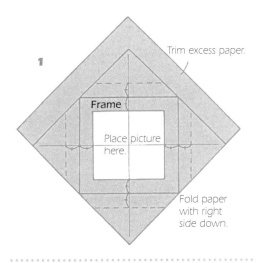

Trim excess paper.

Frame

Place picture here.

Fold paper with right side down.

2

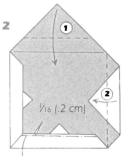

①

②

1/16 (.2 cm)

Double fold the edges to give the frame more body. Fold the top and bottom edges 1/16 inch (.2 cm) longer.

3

Insert your picture or card, then secure it on the back with double-sided tape.

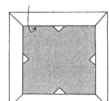

Begin with Square Fold A on page 53.

1

④ ③

② ①

Crease along the dotted line.

2

Open the right flap and flatten as shown in Step 3.

3

③ ② ①

Handkerchief Surprises

Page 27, Projects 1-2

1) Handkerchief/Napkin Flower

MATERIAL: One cloth handkerchief or napkin, size 19 x 19 inches (48.5 x 48.5 cm).

INSTRUCTIONS: Starch the fabric, using either regular starch or iron-on spray starch. If using regular starch, iron the fabric before folding.

4

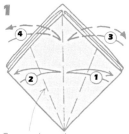

5

Repeat the fold on the left flap. Turn over and repeat.

6

Fold the top flaps in along the dotted line.

7

8

9

Repeat the folds on the remaining flaps.

10

Fold the four flaps down, then open the flower.

11

12

2) Handkerchief/Napkin Crane

MATERIAL: One cloth hand-kerchief or napkin, size 19 x 19 inches (48.5 x 48.5 cm).

INSTRUCTIONS: Starch the fabric, using either regular starch of iron-on spray starch. If using regular starch, iron the fabric before fold-ing.

Begin with Square Fold A on page 53.

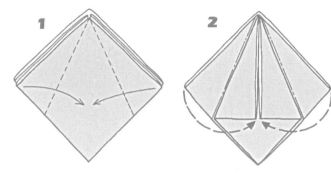

1

2

3

Crease along the horizontal dotted line.

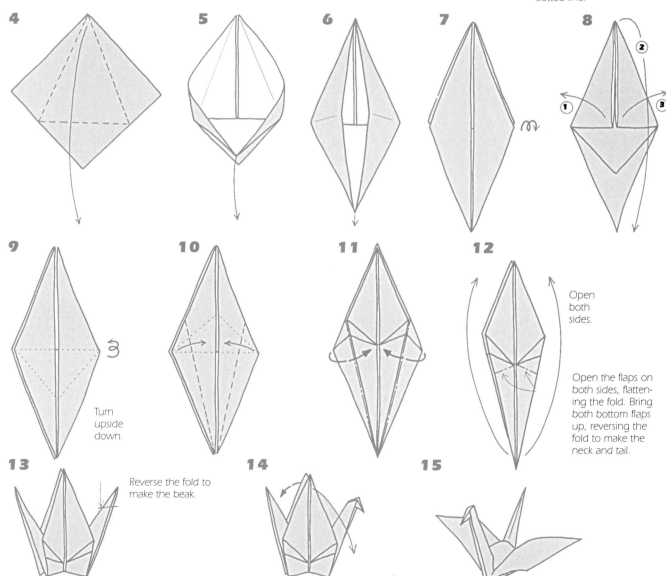

4

5

Turn upside down.

6

7

8

9

10

11

12

Open both sides.

Open the flaps on both sides, flatten-ing the fold. Bring both bottom flaps up, reversing the fold to make the neck and tail.

13

Reverse the fold to make the beak.

14

15

Pages/Photo Holders

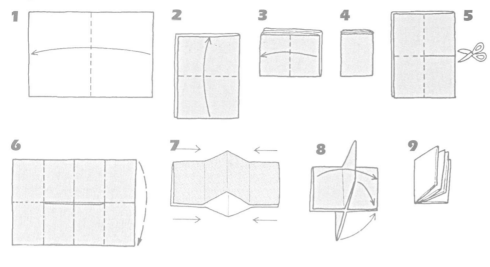

Cover

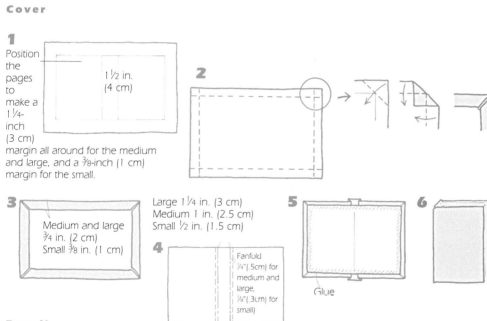

1 Position the pages to make a 1¼-inch (3 cm) margin all around for the medium and large, and a ⅜-inch (1 cm) margin for the small.

1½ in. (4 cm)

Medium and large ¾ in. (2 cm)
Small ⅜ in. (1 cm)

Large 1¼ in. (3 cm)
Medium 1 in. (2.5 cm)
Small ½ in. (1.5 cm)

Fanfold ¼"(.5cm) for medium and large, ⅛"(.3cm) for small)

Glue

Pencil

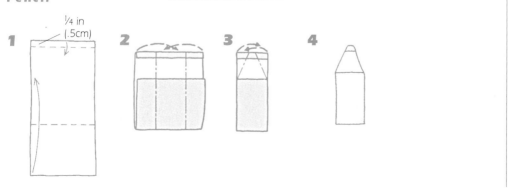

¼ in (.5cm)

Book and Pencil

Page 28, Projects 1-2

1) Pages/Photo Holders and Cover

In addition to paper you will need
Scissors
White craft glue

Paper: For the pages/photo holders use regular paper, size 3 x 5 ½ inches (7.5 x 14 cm) for small; 7 x 16 inches (18 x 40.5 cm) for medium; and 12 x 16 ½ inches (30.5 x 42 cm) for large. For the cover use heavyweight paper, size 2 ½ x 4 ½ inches 6.5 x 11.5 cm) for small; 5 ½ x 11 ½ inches (14 x 29 cm) for medium; and 8 ½ x 12 inches (21.5 x 30.5 cm) for large.

Instructions: If your are making a book with a cover, make the pages/photo holders first, then adjust the size of the cover to fit.

Tip: Without a cover the pages/photo holders can be used as an instant notebook.

Romantic Reminders

Lace Doily Creations

Page 29, Projects 1-3

1) Envelope/Gift Wrapper

In addition to paper you will need: A ribbon, size ⅜ x 16 inches (1 x 40.5 cm)

Paper: Paper doily, size 10½ inches (26.5 cm) in diameter.

Instructions: Fold the envelope around the letter, card, or gift as shown. Thread the ribbon through the holes in the doily to make the closure.

Tip: If you don't have the card or gift you'll be inserting when you make the envelope, use a piece of cardboard cut to the approximate size of the item when folding.

2) Carrier Pigeon

Paper: One-half of a paper doily, size 10 ½ inches (26.5 cm) in diameter.

Instructions: Before beginning Step 1, cut the doily in half.

3) Pigeon with Heart

Paper: Paper doily, size 10 ½ inches (26.5 cm) in diameter. Small piece of red paper.

Instructions: At Step 6, fold the excess inside so that the beak will look neat.

Tip: Try using metallic red paper for the heart for an extra warm glow.

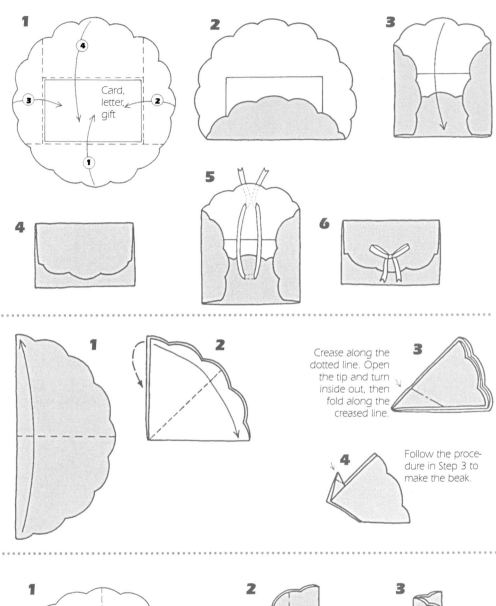

Card, letter, gift

Crease along the dotted line. Open the tip and turn inside out, then fold along the creased line.

Follow the procedure in Step 3 to make the beak.

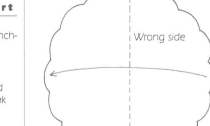

Wrong side

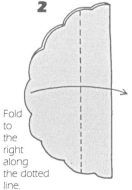

Fold to the right along the dotted line.

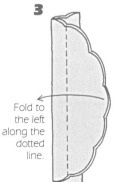

Fold to the left along the dotted line.

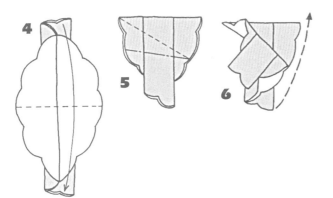

4 **5** **6** **7**

Open the tip and turn inside out to make a beak. (Refer to Step 3 for project 2, the carrier pigeon.)

8 ¾ in. (2 cm) × ½ in. (1.5 cm)

Heart

Cut a heart from the red paper and glue.

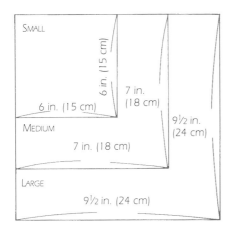

SMALL

6 in. (15 cm)

6 in. (15 cm)

7 in. (18 cm)

MEDIUM

7 in. (18 cm)

9½ in. (24 cm)

LARGE

9½ in. (24 cm)

1 *Begin with Steps 1-7 of project 2, page 86 before proceeding with Step 1.*

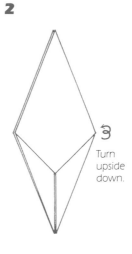

Bring the right upper flap to the left. Turn over and repeat.

2

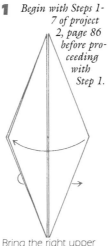

Turn upside down.

Lucky Cranes

Page 30, Projects 1-2

1) Resting Crane

Paper: Use gold or red paper in different sizes to make small, medium, or large cranes. For large, use size 9 ½ x 9 ½ inches (24 x 24 cm); for medium, 7 x 7 inches (18 x 18 cm); and for small, 6 x 6 inches (15 x 15 cm).

Instructions: Begin with Square Fold B on page 53, keeping the colored side out. Then follow Steps 1-7 for Project 2 before proceeding with Step 1 of this project. At Step 9 make sharp folds by creasing well.

3 **4** **5** **6**

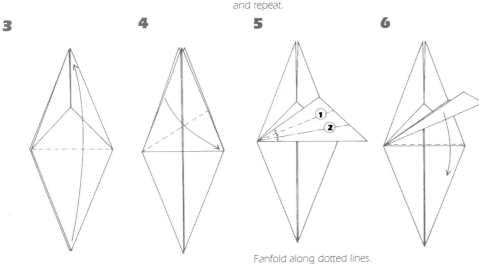

Fanfold along dotted lines.

1) Resting Crane

Continued from page 89.

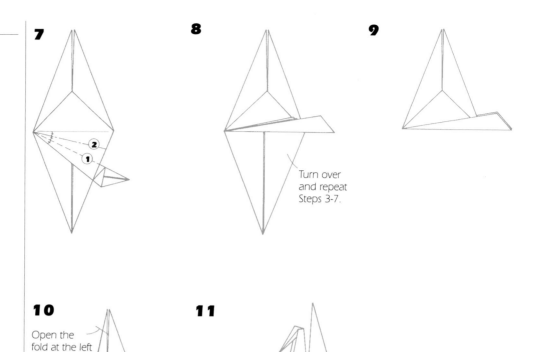

7

8

Turn over
and repeat
Steps 3-7.

9

10

Open the
fold at the left
tip, push and
reverse the
fold to make
a beak.

11

2) Flying Crane

Paper: Use gold or red paper in different sizes to make small, medium, or large cranes. For large, use 9 ½ x 9 ½ inches (24 x 24 cm); for medium, 7 x 7 inches (18 x 18 cm); and for small, 6 x 6 inches (15 x 15 cm).

Instructions: Begin with Square Fold B on page 53, keeping the colored side out, before proceeding with Step 1 of this project.

Begin with Square Fold B on page 53, working with the colored side out.

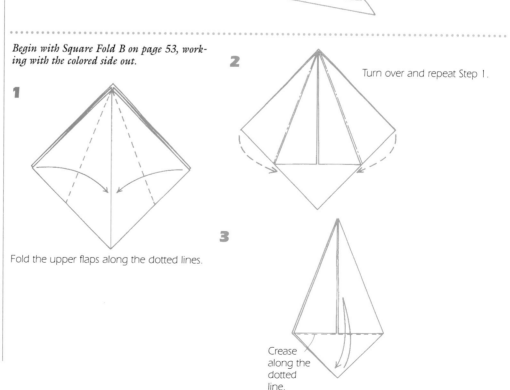

1

Fold the upper flaps along the dotted lines.

2

Turn over and repeat Step 1.

3

Crease along the dotted line.

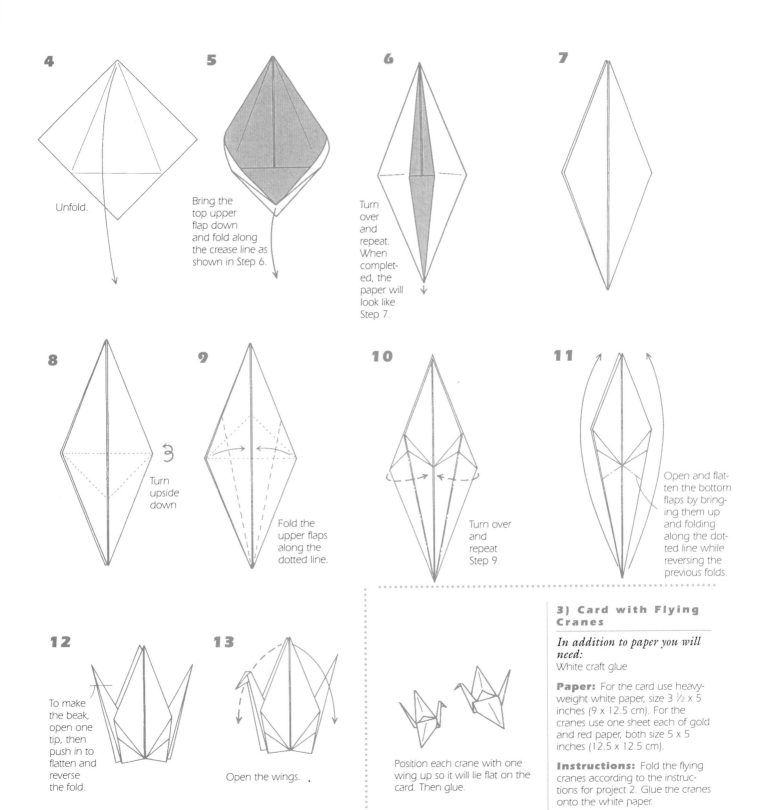

4

Unfold.

5

Bring the top upper flap down and fold along the crease line as shown in Step 6.

6

Turn over and repeat. When completed, the paper will look like Step 7.

7

8

Turn upside down

9

Fold the upper flaps along the dotted line.

10

Turn over and repeat Step 9.

11

Open and flatten the bottom flaps by bringing them up and folding along the dotted line while reversing the previous folds.

12

To make the beak, open one tip, then push in to flatten and reverse the fold.

13

Open the wings.

Position each crane with one wing up so it will lie flat on the card. Then glue.

3) Card with Flying Cranes

In addition to paper you will need:
White craft glue

Paper: For the card use heavyweight white paper, size 3 ½ x 5 inches (9 x 12.5 cm). For the cranes use one sheet each of gold and red paper, both size 5 x 5 inches (12.5 x 12.5 cm).

Instructions: Fold the flying cranes according to the instructions for project 2. Glue the cranes onto the white paper.

Book Covers and Bookmarks

Page 31, Projects 1-4

1) Newspaper Book Cover

In addition to paper you will need:
White craft glue
Gift wrap

Paper: Newspaper or gift wrap-paper in a size large enough to cover the book. Heavyweight black paper, enough to make four rectangles for the corner reinforcements.

Instructions: Fold the paper as shown in Step1 and place the open book on it. Crease the paper at all the book's outer edges. Trim any excess. You may not want to glue the book's front and back cover to the book cover flaps. At Step 2 and 3, do not glue the flaps but slip the book's covers into the flaps and disregard Step 6. Refer to project 3, page 89. At Step 4, cut the rectangles so they will fit as shown when folded, then glue.

2) Hat and Shirt Bookmark

In addition to paper you will need:
White craft glue

Paper: Heavyweight black paper, size 2 ½ inches (6.5 x 6.5 cm). Satin ribbon, size ½ x 10 inches (1.5 x 25.5 cm).

Instructions:
Punch a hole at the center top of the black paper and insert and tie ribbon. Glue the completed hat and shirt to the paper.

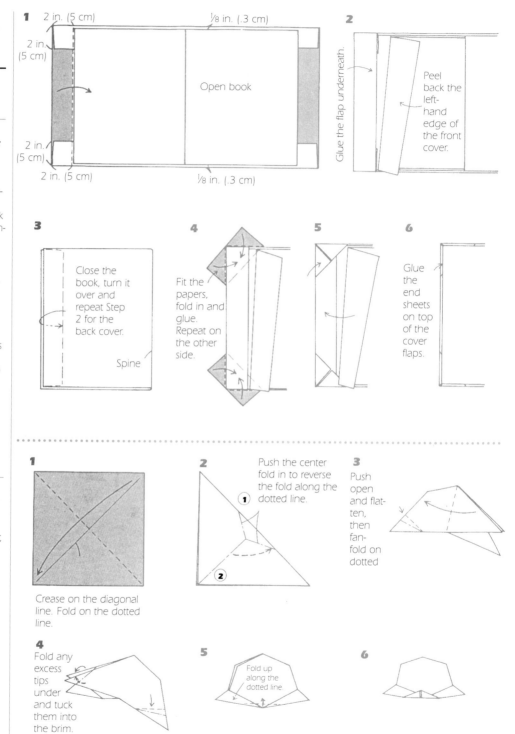

1 2 in. (5 cm) ⅛ in. (.3 cm)
2 in. (5 cm)
Open book
2 in. (5 cm)
2 in. (5 cm)
2 in. (5 cm) ⅛ in. (.3 cm)

2 Glue the flap underneath. Peel back the left-hand edge of the front cover.

3 Close the book, turn it over and repeat Step 2 for the back cover. Spine

4 Fit the papers, fold in and glue. Repeat on the other side.

5

6 Glue the end sheets on top of the cover flaps.

1 Crease on the diagonal line. Fold on the dotted line.

2 Push the center fold in to reverse the fold along the dotted line.

3 Push open and flatten, then fanfold on dotted

4 Fold any excess tips under and tuck them into the brim.

5 Fold up along the dotted line

6

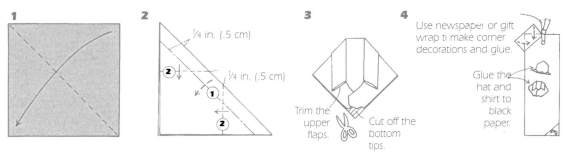

1

2

¼ in. (.5 cm)

¼ in. (.5 cm)

② ① ② ①

3

Trim the upper flaps.

Cut off the bottom tips.

4

Use newspaper or gift wrap ti make corner decorations and glue.

Glue the hat and shirt to black paper.

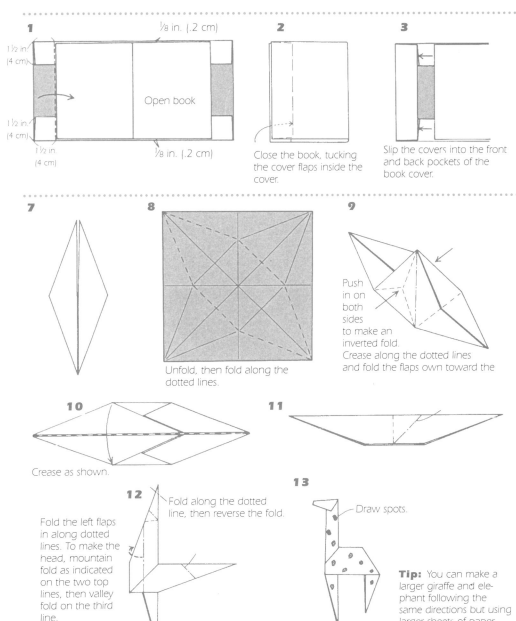

1

⅛ in. (.2 cm)

1½ in. (4 cm)

1½ in. (4 cm)

1½ in. (4 cm)

Open book

⅛ in. (.2 cm)

2

Close the book, tucking the cover flaps inside the cover.

3

Slip the covers into the front and back pockets of the book cover.

3) Gift-Wrap Book Cover.

Paper: Gift-wrap paper in a size large enough to cover the book.

Instructions: Cover the book with the paper as shown and crease around the book.

4) Giraffe and Elephant Bookmark

7

8

Unfold, then fold along the dotted lines.

9

Push in on both sides to make an inverted fold. Crease along the dotted lines and fold the flaps own toward the

In addition to paper you will need: Satin Ribbon, ½ x 10 inches (1.5 x 25.5 cm)

Paper: For the bookmark use heavyweight paper in a solid color of your choice, size 2 x 6 inches (5 x 15 cm). For the giraffe use regular-weight paper, size 6 x 6 inches (15 x 15 cm). For the elephant use regular-weight paper, size 2½ x 4 ½ inches (6.5 x 11.5 cm).

10

Crease as shown.

11

Instructions: For the giraffe, begin with Square Fold B on page 53. Then follow Steps 1-6 for project 2, page 86-87 (Lucky Cranes) before continuing with Steps 7-13 of this project. At Step 11 for the giraffe, crease as shown, then flatten the left-hand fold, bringing it up along the center crease line. Push the right-hand side in along the diagonal fold, folding up along the center crease line, then continue with Step 12. For the bookmark, punch a hole at the center top of the heavyweight paper and insert and tie the ribbon. Glue the completed giraffe and elephant .

12

Fold the left flaps in along dotted lines. To make the head, mountain fold as indicated on the two top lines, then valley fold on the third line.

Fold along the dotted line, then reverse the fold.

13

Draw spots.

Tip: You can make a larger giraffe and elephant following the same directions but using larger sheets of paper.

Elephant

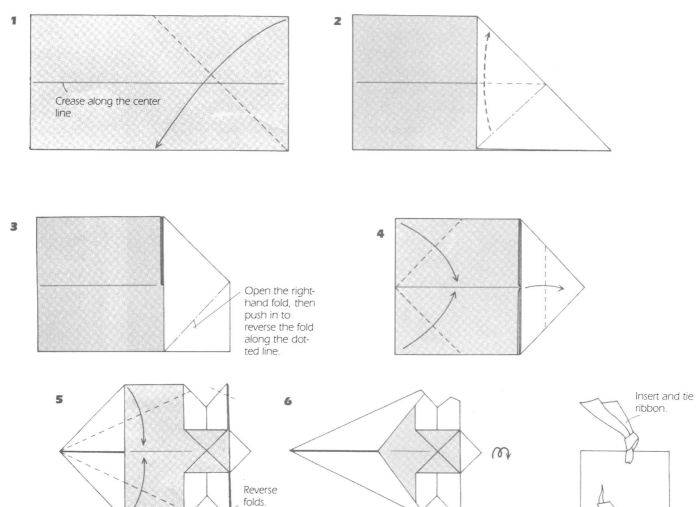

1 Crease along the center line.

2

3 Open the right-hand fold, then push in to reverse the fold along the dotted line.

4

5 Reverse folds.

6

7 Fanfold along the dotted lines.

① ②

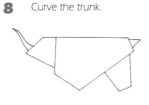

8 Curve the trunk.

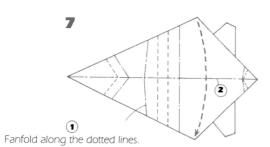

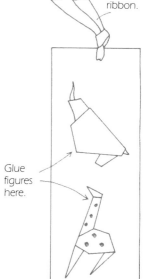

Insert and tie ribbon.

Glue figures here.

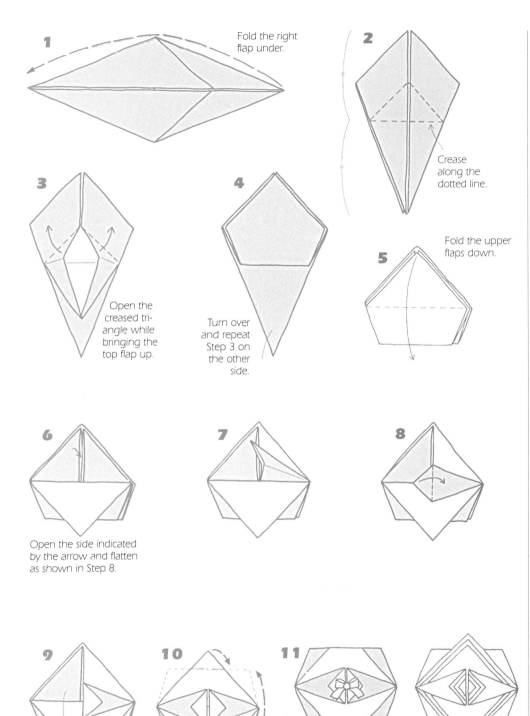

1 Fold the right flap under.

2 Crease along the dotted line.

3 Open the creased triangle while bringing the top flap up.

4 Turn over and repeat Step 3 on the other side.

5 Fold the upper flaps down.

6 Open the side indicated by the arrow and flatten as shown in Step 8.

7

8

9 Follow the same procedure on the left.

10

11 If desired, use a ribbon as a closure (as shown for the larger container on page 32).

Japanese Design

Page 32, Projects 1-7

1) Small-Item Containers

In addition to paper you will need:
White craft glue
Ribbon for a closure (optional)

Paper: One sheet of patterned paper and two sheets of solid-color paper, all size 6 x 6 inches (15 x 15 cm) for the larger container. You can use only two sheets of paper or add a third for more color. In making a small container with three colors like the one shown on page 32, cut one of the solid-color sheet ¼ inch (.6 cm) smaller than the printed sheet.

Instructions: Lay the papers on top of each other with the right sides facing out. Glue the papers together and allow to dry before folding, then fold as one.

Begin with these directions for folding the paper so it will look like the figure in Step 1. Fold the paper in half crosswise to form a triangle, then unfold. Position the paper so the print side is facing down and the crease is horizontal. Bring the bottom point of the lower triangle to the center fold and crease. Bring the top point of the upper triangle to the center fold and crease. Do not unfold. You should have formed a "new" upper and lower triangle. Now bring the bottom point of the new lower triangle to the center fold and crease. Bring the top point of the new upper triangle to the center fold and crease. Slightly open these last two folds and by pushing from underneath, invert the two folds, and crease. This should bring the flaps from the first two triangles to the top and the result should look Step 1. Continue following Steps 1-11.

2) Sewing Container

In addition to paper you will need:
2 buttons, size ⅜ inch (1 cm) in diameter
Embroidery thread

Paper: One sheet printed paper and one sheet of solid-color paper, each size 6 x 6 inches (15 x 15 cm).

Instructions: Place the papers on top of each other with the right sides facing out. When the folding is complete, use a heavy book or object as a weight for pressing the creases in place. Once you've attached the buttons with the embroidery thread, cut the thread but leave a 6-inch (15-cm) tail on one side. You will use this thread o open the container.

Begin with the Four-Corner Fold A on page 52.

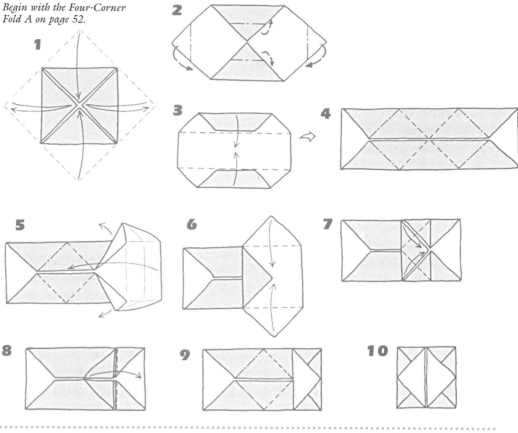

3) Two-Style Container

Paper: One sheet printed paper and one sheet solid-color paper, both size 6 ½ x 6 ½ inches (16.5 x 16.5 cm).

Instructions: Crease well at Step 6; this will make it easier to open.

Tip: At Steps 8 you can create two styles of this container by leaving the flaps open as shown in Step 9 or folding them in as shown in Step 10.

Start with Square Fold B on page 53.

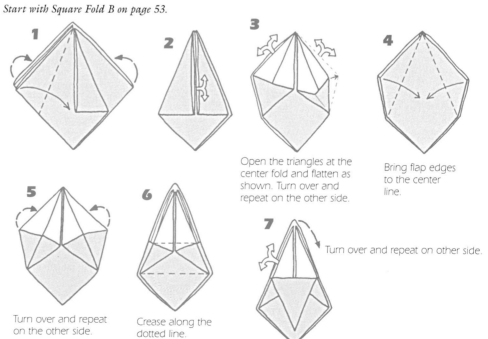

3 Open the triangles at the center fold and flatten as shown. Turn over and repeat on the other side.

4 Bring flap edges to the center line.

5 Turn over and repeat on the other side.

6 Crease along the dotted line.

7 Turn over and repeat on other side.

8

Bring the peaks down and fold as shown in the diagram.

9

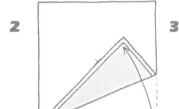

10

4-5) Coin Purses— Two Variations

Paper: For project 4 use one sheet printed paper and one sheet white paper, both size 6 x 6 inches (15 x 15 cm). For project 5 use two sheets of printed paper, size 6 x 6 inches (15 x 15 cm).

Instructions: Place the two sheets of paper for your chosen project on top of each other. Folding as one, crease to make an x in the center of the papers. Trim the sides of the paper that will become the outside of the finished purse (in illustrations, it's the paper shown underneath the top sheet) ¼ inch (.6 cm) to ⅜ inch (1 cm). This exposes the paper underneath and becomes the border. Use the x crease to center the papers. Continue folding as one, following the steps for your chosen project.

(4)

1

Crease an x at the center of each paper.

2

Bring the bottom edge up and place on an imaginary line connecting the left corner and the center, then fold.

3

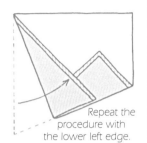

Repeat the procedure with the lower left edge.

4

Repeat the procedure with the upper left edge.

5

Repeat the procedure with the upper right edge, then unfold.

Fold again, placing the right flap on top and tucking the excess paper inside.

6

Make sure that all the corners are placed on top.

(5)

1

Crease and trim paper as for 4, then place papers on top of each other.

From the bottom left corner, measure toward the center 1½ inches (3.5 cm). From this point, bring the bottom edge up and place on an imaginary line connecting the point with the center, then fold.

2

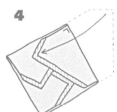

Repeat the procedure for folding the left edge, making sure that the corner made by the two folds is a right angle.

3

Repeat Step 2.

4

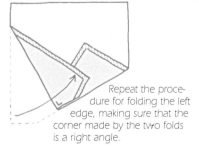

Make sure that each edge touches the center when folded.

5

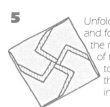

Unfold the flap on top and fold again, placing the right-hand corner of the first fold on top and tucking the excess paper inside.

ORIGAMI

6) Coaster

Paper: Print or solid-color paper, size 1½ x 7 inches (3.5 x 18 cm)

Instructions: Steps 1-3 shows you how to fold an equilateral triangle. Repeat these Steps until you get to the end of the paper. Unfold, to make the hexagon as shown.

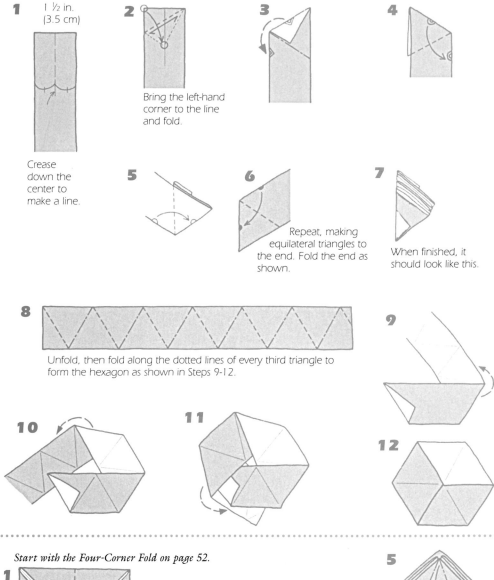

1 1 ½ in. (3.5 cm)

Crease down the center to make a line.

2 Bring the left-hand corner to the line and fold.

3

4

5

6 Repeat, making equilateral triangles to the end. Fold the end as shown.

7 When finished, it should look like this.

8 Unfold, then fold along the dotted lines of every third triangle to form the hexagon as shown in Steps 9-12.

9

10

11

12

7) Container for Small Items

In addition to paper you will need: White craft glue

Paper: One sheet of printed paper and solid-color paper, both size 6 x 6 inches (15 x 15 cm).

Instructions: Place the papers on top of each other with the right sides facing out. Glue together, letting the glue dry completely before folding. Crease well at each step. At Step 2, fold as shown to make the center line. Fold forward along the diagonal dotted line and unfold.

(continued on page 95)

Start with the Four-Corner Fold on page 52.

1

2

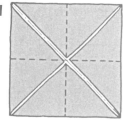

3

4

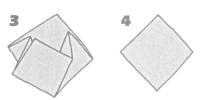

5

Crease along the dotted lines to make the triangle shown. Open the top flap and fold down along the horizontal dotted line. Bring the side flaps from that fold to the center.

ORIGAMI

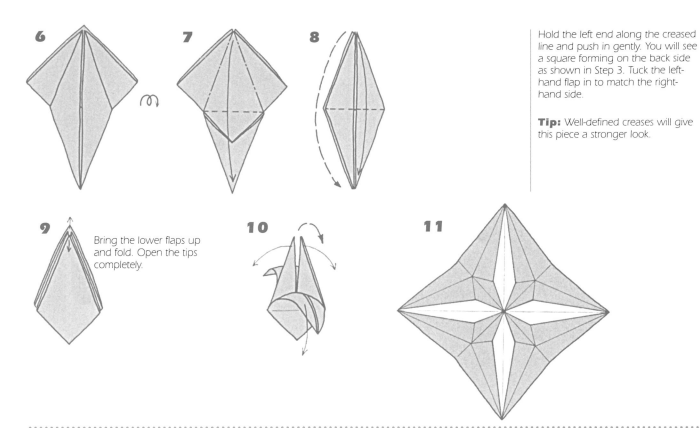

6

7

8

Hold the left end along the creased line and push in gently. You will see a square forming on the back side as shown in Step 3. Tuck the left-hand flap in to match the right-hand side.

Tip: Well-defined creases will give this piece a stronger look.

9

Bring the lower flaps up and fold. Open the tips completely.

10

11

BOXES AND CONTAINERS

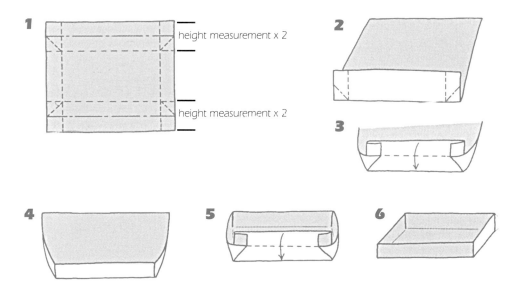

1

height measurement x 2

height measurement x 2

2

3

4

5

6

Drawer Dividers

Page 33

Paper: Use heavyweight paper in colors of your choice.

Instructions: Determine the size of the divider by the items it will hold. Figure the dimensions of the finished bottom side. Figure the height for your finished container. Add the measurements for the finished height to the measurements for the bottom side. If you are making a rectangular-shaped divider, double the measurement for the height on each of the long sides of the flat rectangle before folding. If you are making a square-shaped divider, double the measurement for the height on two opposite sides of the flat square before folding.

Tip: For neat storage, make all the dividers that will be used together the same height.

Recycled Bins

Page 34

Paper: Old newspapers. Use full-size newspaper sheets for large containers and smaller sheets for smaller containers. You can also cut the newspaper to make a variety of smaller sizes. If you do this, cut the paper along the unfolded edges, making sure you always cut the paper into a rectangle rather than a square.

Instructions: Place the folded sheet lengthwise. Fold it in half, then fold the upper flap down along a line one-third the measurement of the folded sheet. At Step 3, fold up along the dotted line, making sure that the edges are aligned. At Step 7, crease well along the dotted lines.

1

Folded edge

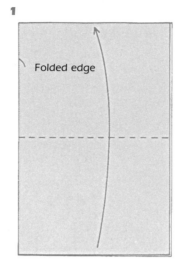

2 Fold down along the dotted line that is $\frac{1}{3}$ the measurement of the folded sheet.

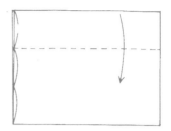

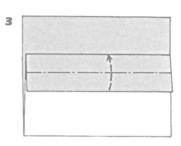

3

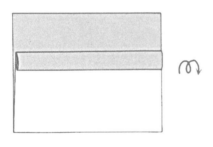

4

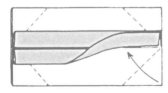

5 Turn over and repeat Steps 2 and 3 on the other side.

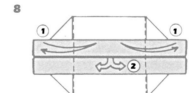

6

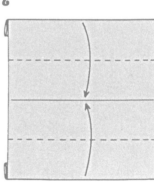

7

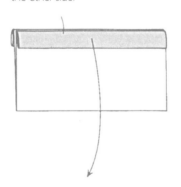

Fold the four corners in along the dotted lines, tucking them underneath the folds as shown.

8

9

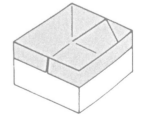

Bottom

1
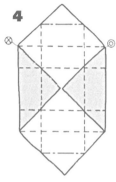 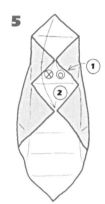

2
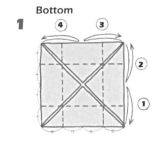

Fold horizontally so that both sides meet in the middle, then unfold.

3

Fold vertically so that both sides meet in the middle, then unfold.

4

Unfold the top and bottom of the triangles.

5
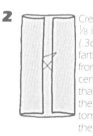

Bring the x and o together, then fold the top flap to cover.

6
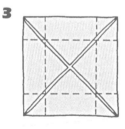

Repeat Step 5 on the other side.

7

Top

1
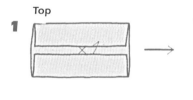

2

Crease ⅛ in (.3cm) farther from the center than for the bottom of the box.

3

1
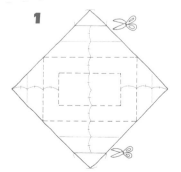

2 **Bottom**
 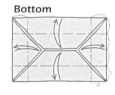

3 **Top**
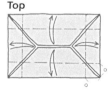

4
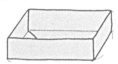

Marbleized Gift Boxes

Page 36, Projects 1-2

1) Square Box

Paper: Marbleized paper, sizes 9 ½ x 9 ½ inches (24 x 24 cm); 7 x 7 inches (18 x 18 cm); 6 x 6 inches (15 x 15 cm).

Instructions: For the bottom of the box, start with the Four-Corner Fold on page 52. Follow steps 1-7. For the top of the box, follow Steps 1-7 given for the bottom of the box with one exception. You will need to make the top of the box slightly larger than the bottom so it will fit over the bottom. To do this, follow Steps 1-2 given for the top of the box, creasing each line ⅛ inch (.3 cm) farther from the center than the crease lines given for the bottom of the box.

Tip: Steps 2 and 3 for the bottom of the box form the inner square of the box; crease carefully for well-defined lines.

2) Rectangular Box

In addition to paper you will need: Scissors

Paper: Marbleized paper, size 7 x 7 inches (18 x 18 cm).

Instructions: You will be following the same basic procedures for the square box, project 1, with several modifications. Begin by measuring 1 ½ inches (4 cm) from the tip of two opposite corners of the square. Cut off each tip at this point as indicated in Step 1. When the tips are off, fold the ends with the cut-off tips to the center first, then fold the other ends toward the center as shown in Step 2. Proceed with Step 2, referring to Steps 4-7 for the square box, project 1. Remember to make the top slightly larger so it will fit over the bottom by creasing the lines for the top ⅛ inch (.3 cm) farther from the center than the crease lines for the bottom.

BASIC BOX INSTRUCTIONS

Begin with Four-Corner Fold on page 52.

1

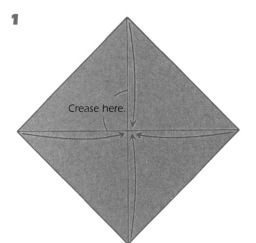

Crease here.

2

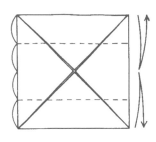

Crease along the dotted line.

3

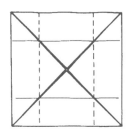

Crease along the dotted line.

4

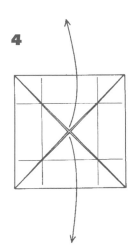

5

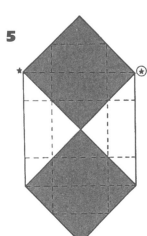

6

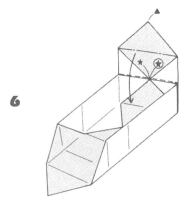

7

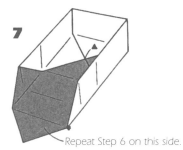

Repeat Step 6 on this side.

8

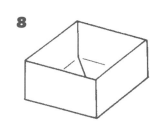

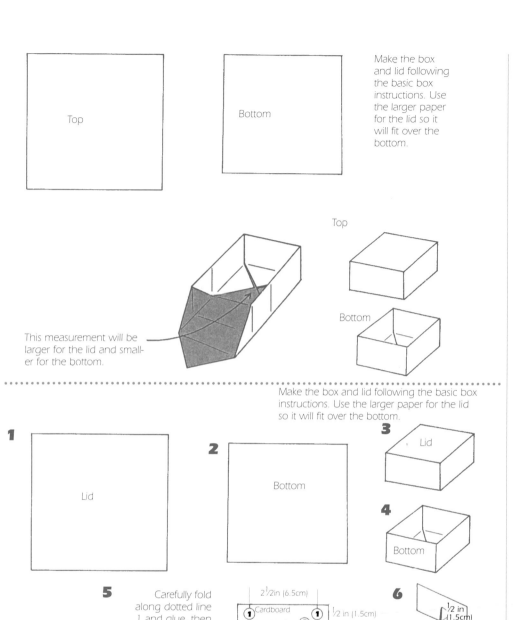

Top

Bottom

Make the box
and lid following
the basic box
instructions. Use
the larger paper
for the lid so it
will fit over the
bottom.

Top

Bottom

This measurement will be
larger for the lid and smaller for the bottom.

Make the box and lid following the basic box
instructions. Use the larger paper for the lid
so it will fit over the bottom.

1

Lid

2

Bottom

3

Lid

4

Bottom

5 Carefully fold
along dotted line
1 and glue, then
fold and glue
along dotted line
2. Cut on dotted
line 3.

2½in (6.5cm)

① Cardboard ①

② ②

③

② ②

3in (7.5cm)

½ in (1.5cm)

1in (2cm)

1in (2cm)

½ in (1.5cm)

3in (7.5cm)

6

½ in
(1.5cm)

½ in
(1.5cm)

Make a divider for the
inside of the box, then
make ribbons, a flower
or bow to decorate
the outside.

7a

⅜in (1cm)

Make three separate
rounds with paper
strips and arrange to
make a flower shape.
Glue the flower to the
ribbons' crossing point.

Cut strips from contrasting-color
paper to make ribbons.

7b

Use a strip of paper to
make the ends of the
bow, glue to the rib-
bon, then glue the
bow on top.

Make two separate rounds
with paper strips and
arrange to make a bow

Glue ribbons on opposite
corners of the box.

Gift-Wrap Boxes

Page 37, Projects 1-2

1) Large Box with Lid

Paper: Two sheets of heavyweight gift-wrap paper, one size 18
x 18 inches (45.5 x 45.5 cm), the
other size 17 ½ x 17 ½ inches
(44.5 x 44.5 cm).

Instructions: Follow the basic
box instructions on page 98, making a bottom and lid. Use the larger sheet of paper for the lid so it
will fit over the bottom.

Tip: Experiment with different patterns and colors of wrapping paper
for some interesting effects.

2) Small Box with Lid

*In addition to paper you will
need:*
White craft glue
Scissors

Paper: Two sheets of heavyweight gift-wrap paper, one size 6
x 6 inches (15 x 15 cm), the other
size 5 ½ x 5 ½ inches (14 x 14 cm).
Cardboard (for the divider), size 3 x
3 inches (7.5 x 7.5 cm). Use contrasting-color paper to cut pieces
for the ribbons and bows.

Instructions: Follow the basic
box instructions on page 98, making a bottom and a lid. Use the
larger sheet of paper for the lid so it
will fit over the bottom.

Tip: Experiment with different patterns and colors of wrapping paper
for some interesting effects.

(Continued from page 99)

Alternate Fold for a Cube-Shaped Box
Begin with Four-Corner Fold A on page 52

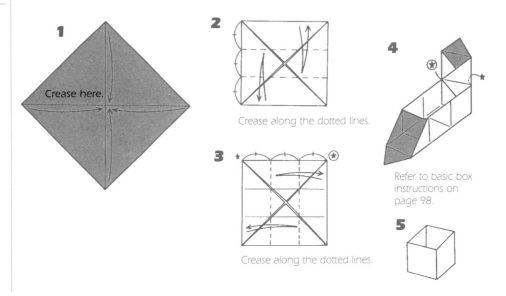

1

Crease here.

2

Crease along the dotted lines.

3

Crease along the dotted lines.

4

Refer to basic box instructions on page 98.

5

Candy Box

Page 38

Paper: Two sheets of heavy-weight printed paper, one size 19 x 19 inches (48.5 x 48.5 cm) and one size 19 ¾ x 19 ¾ inches (50 x 50 cm). Four sheets of heavy-weight black paper, all size 11 x 11 inches (28 x 28 cm).

Instructions: Refer to the instructions for folding a basic box on page 98. Use the larger sheet of printed paper for the lid so it will fit over the bottom. Make the bottom of the box first.

Tip: the inner boxes will be ½ inch (1.5 cm) less in depth than the bottom of the outer box.

Outer box.

1

2 in. (5 cm)

Refer to instructions for folding a basic box on page 000.

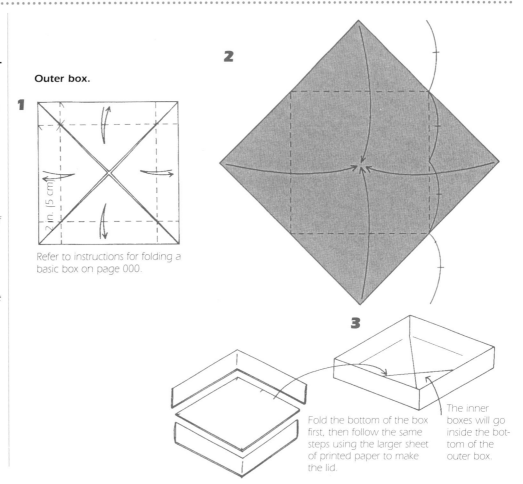

2

3

Fold the bottom of the box first, then follow the same steps using the larger sheet of printed paper to make the lid.

The inner boxes will go inside the bottom of the outer box.

Inner box

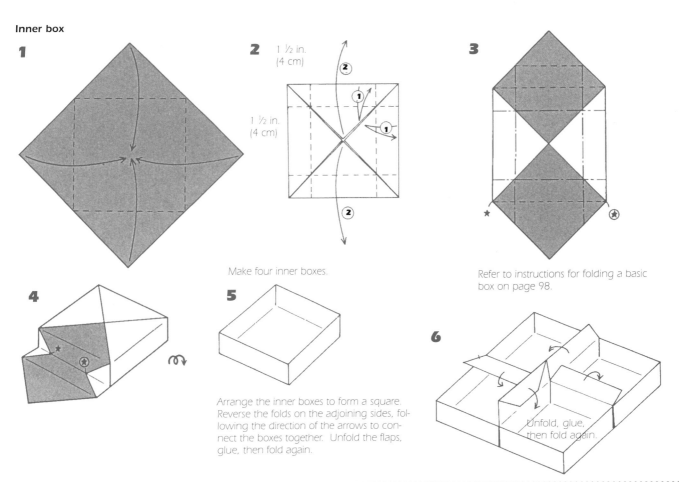

1

2 1 ½ in.
(4 cm)

1 ½ in.
(4 cm)

Make four inner boxes.

3

Refer to instructions for folding a basic box on page 98.

4

5

Arrange the inner boxes to form a square. Reverse the folds on the adjoining sides, following the direction of the arrows to connect the boxes together. Unfold the flaps, glue, then fold again.

6

Unfold, glue, then fold again.

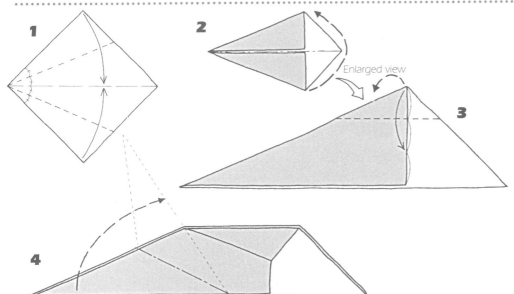

1

2

Enlarged view

3

4

Crease well along the dotted line. Open, flatten, and reverse the left hand triangle and crease again.

Swan Container

Page 39

Paper: Medium to heavyweight paper, size 12 ½ x 12 ½ inches (32 x 32 cm).

Instructions: Follow Steps 1-11. At Step 3, the fold at the dotted line is the back of the swan. For Steps 5 and 6, refer to page 51 for the basic directions for reversing folds.

Tip: Using heavy paper will give you a stronger container.

Swan Container

Continued from page 101

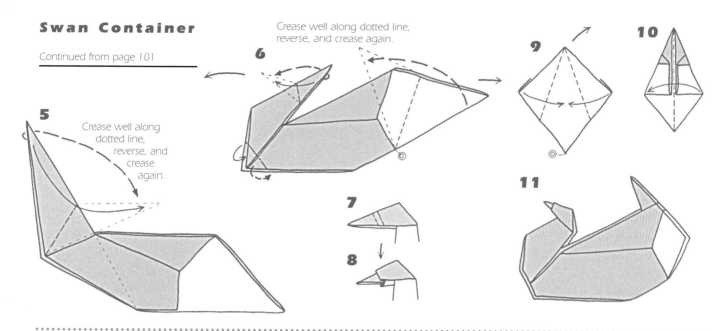

6 Crease well along dotted line, reverse, and crease again.

5 Crease well along dotted line, reverse, and crease again.

9

10

7

8

11

Recycled Containers

Paper Vase and Dustpan

Page 35, Projects 1-2

1) Calendar Container

In addition to paper you will need:
White craft glue

Paper: Old calendar pages, size approximately 28 x 28 inches (71 x 71 cm) for the larger container; and approximately 21 x 21 inches (53.5 x 53.5 cm) for the smaller container.

Instructions: At Step 6, unfold, then glue the fold of the triangle marked with the star. Fold the top flaps along the dotted lines so that the glued triangle goes underneath. Repeat this procedure on the remaining three sides.

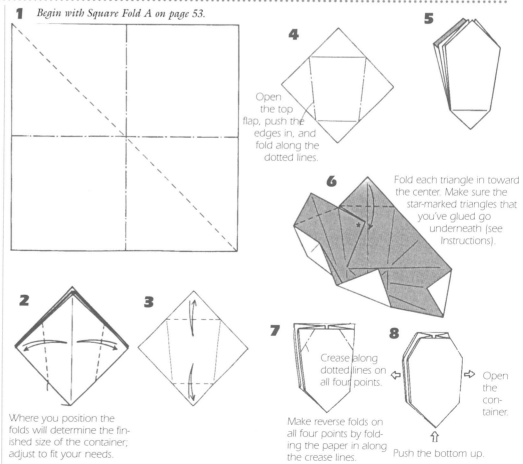

1 Begin with Square Fold A on page 53.

2 Where you position the folds will determine the finished size of the container; adjust to fit your needs.

3

4 Open the top flap, push the edges in, and fold along the dotted lines.

5

6 Fold each triangle in toward the center. Make sure the star-marked triangles that you've glued go underneath (see Instructions).

7 Crease along dotted lines on all four points.

Make reverse folds on all four points by folding the paper in along the crease lines.

8 Open the container.

Push the bottom up.

9

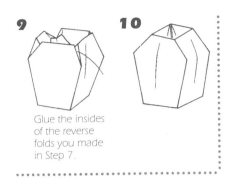

10

Glue the insides of the reverse folds you made in Step 7.

Fold on the dotted line as shown to bring the corner past the center point.

2

3

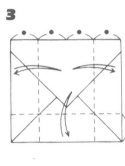

4

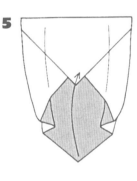

5

6

2) Dustpan

Paper: Two full-size newspaper sheets.

Instructions: you will be folding four layers of paper as one. At Step 3, crease well.

1

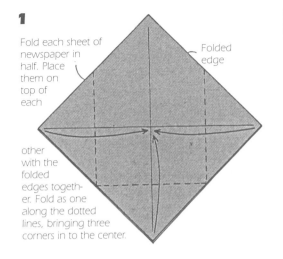

Fold each sheet of newspaper in half. Place them on top of each

Folded edge

other with the folded edges together. Fold as one along the dotted lines, bringing three corners in to the center.

A

2

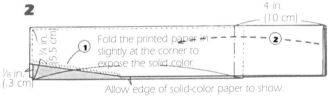

4 in. (10 cm)

Fold the printed paper in slightly at the corner to expose the solid color.

2 ¼ in. (5.5 cm)

⅛ in. (.3 cm)

Allow edge of solid-color paper to show.

Allow edge of printed paper to show.

1

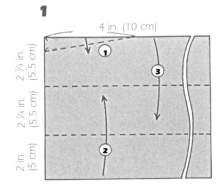

4 in. (10 cm)

2 ¼ in. (5.5 cm)

2 ¼ in. (5.5 cm)

2 in. (5 cm)

3

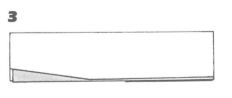

Organizers

Page 41, Projects1-7

1) Rectangular Holder-A

In addition to paper you will need:
White craft glue

Paper: Printed paper, size 6½ x 13 inches (16.5 x 33 cm). Solid-color paper, size 2 ¼ x 9 ½ inches (5.5 x 24 cm).

Instructions: Fold the printed paper, following Step 1. Insert the solid-color paper before folding the right-hand flap back as shown in Step 2.

2) Envelope-B

In addition to paper you will need:
White craft glue

Paper: Printed paper, size 9¼ x 7½ inches (23.5 x 19 cm). Solid-color paper, size 2 ½ x 7 ½ inches (6.5 x 19 cm).

Instructions: Always fold along the dotted lines in the order indicated. Insert the solid-color paper, then glue along the slashed lines and fold backward along the dotted lines as shown in Step 2.

3) Rectangular Holder-C

In addition to paper you will need:
White craft glue

Paper: Printed papers, size 5 x 5½ inches (12.5 x 14 cm). Solid-color papers, size 1¾ x 4¾ inches (4.5 x 12 cm).

Instructions: Choose solid-color papers to match the printed papers. Glue the solid-color paper to the printed paper.

4) Rectangular Holder-D

In addition to paper you will need:
White craft glue

Paper: Printed paper, size 6 x 14½ inches (15 x 37 cm). White paper, size 1 ¾ x 14 ½ inches (4.5 x 37 cm).

Instructions: Fold the printed paper, insert the white paper, then glue both ends. Fold over to create a "knot" as shown in Step 4 and 5.

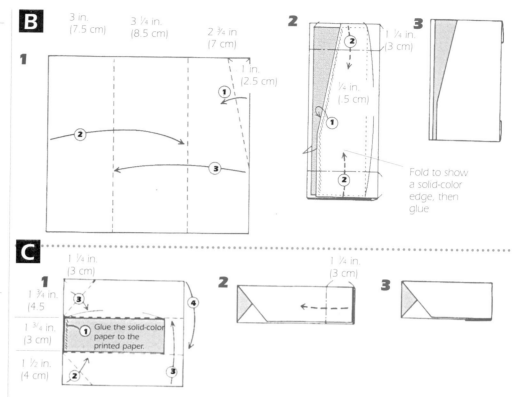

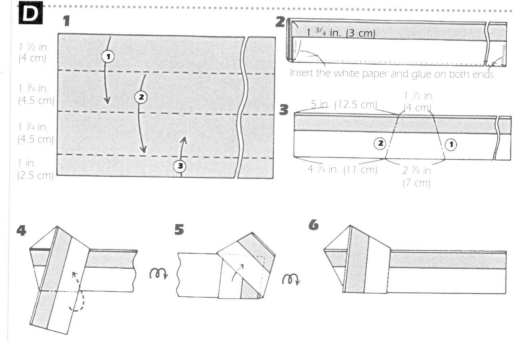

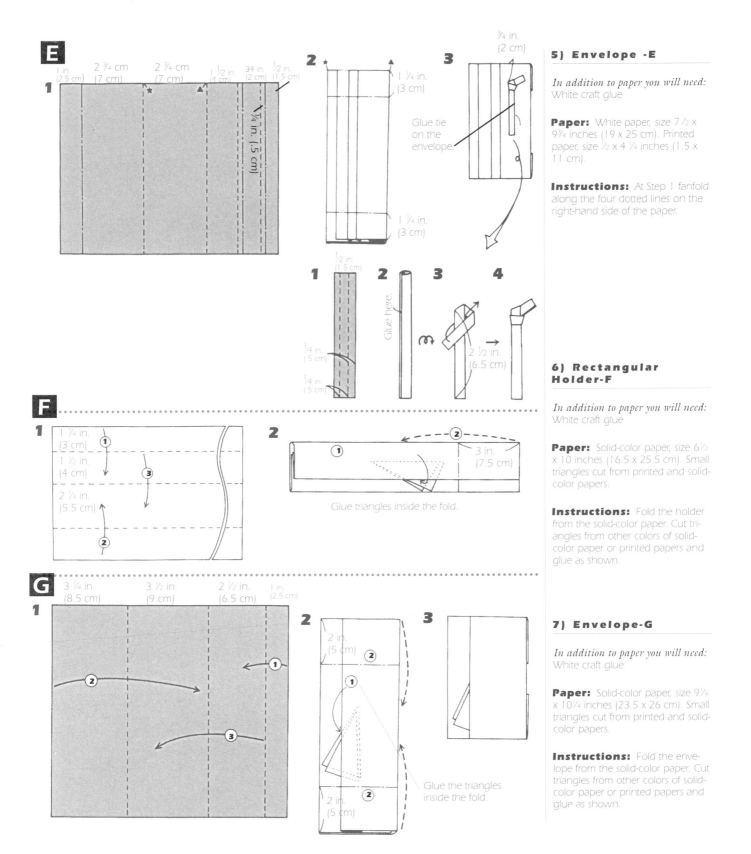

E

1

1 in. (2.5 cm) | 2 ¾ cm (7 cm) | 2 ¾ cm (7 cm) | 1 ½ in. (4 cm) | ¾ in. (2 cm) | ½ in. (1.5 cm)

¼ in. (.5 cm)

2 ★ ▲

1 ¼ in. (3 cm)

1 ¼ in. (3 cm)

3 ¾ in. (2 cm)

Glue tie on the envelope.

1 ½ in. (1.5 cm)

¼ in. (.5 cm)

¼ in. (.5 cm)

Glue here.

2

3 ↻

4

2 ½ in. (6.5 cm)

5) Envelope -E

In addition to paper you will need: White craft glue

Paper: White paper, size 7 ½ x 9¾ inches (19 x 25 cm). Printed paper, size ½ x 4 ¼ inches (1.5 x 11 cm).

Instructions: At Step 1 fanfold along the four dotted lines on the right-hand side of the paper.

F

1

1 ¼ in. (3 cm) ①

1 ½ in. (4 cm) ③

2 ¼ in. (5.5 cm)

②

2

② 3 in. (7.5 cm)

①

Glue triangles inside the fold.

6) Rectangular Holder-F

In addition to paper you will need: White craft glue

Paper: Solid-color paper, size 6½ x 10 inches (16.5 x 25.5 cm). Small triangles cut from printed and solid-color papers.

Instructions: Fold the holder from the solid-color paper. Cut triangles from other colors of solid-color paper or printed papers and glue as shown.

G

1

3 ¼ in. (8.5 cm) | 3 ½ in (9 cm) | 2 ½ in. (6.5 cm) | 1 in. (2.5 cm)

① ② ③

2

2 in. (5 cm) ②

①

2 in. (5 cm) ②

3

Glue the triangles inside the fold.

7) Envelope-G

In addition to paper you will need: White craft glue

Paper: Solid-color paper, size 9¼ x 10¼ inches (23.5 x 26 cm). Small triangles cut from printed and solid-color papers.

Instructions: Fold the envelope from the solid-color paper. Cut triangles from other colors of solid-color paper or printed papers and glue as shown.

Traveling Companions

Page 40, Projects 1-3

1) Wallet

Paper: Medium-weight wrapping paper. The size of the item will determine the size of the paper you will use.

Instructions: Fold around the bills, tickets, etc. As shown in Step 1. At Step 3, fold diagonally on both sides, then reverse both folds in Step 4 to show the denomination of the bills.

Tip: If you do not have the actual currency or items, use a piece of cardboard or paper cut to the approximate size of the item.

2) Handkerchief Case

Paper: Medium-weight gift-wrap, size 20 x 12 ½ inches (53 x 31.5 cm).

Instructions: At Step 1, fold the two opposite short ends of the rectangle in ½ inch (1.5 cm). Follow the remaining steps to complete.

Tip: This container is durable because it's folded into a double layer. By using different sizes of paper, you can make a variety of cases to meet your needs.

3) Tissue Case

Paper: One solid-color sheet of heavy paper and one sheet of gift-wrap paper, both size 13 x 13 inches (33 x 33 cm).

Instructions: Place the papers on top of each other with the heavyweight, solid-colored paper on the top (this will become the inside of the case) then fold as one. Steps 1-5 show how to fold the paper symmetrically. At Step 5, the sizes of the triangles can change depending on the posi-

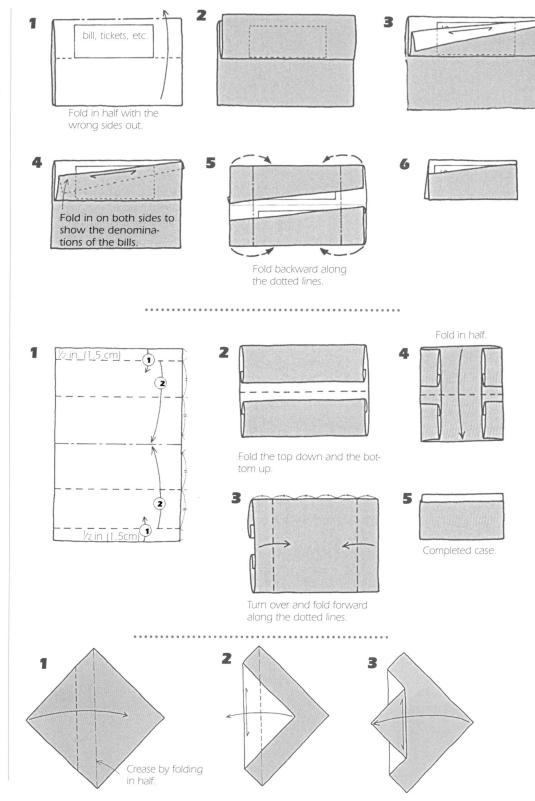

1 bill, tickets, etc.

Fold in half with the wrong sides out.

2

3

4 Fold in on both sides to show the denominations of the bills.

5 Fold backward along the dotted lines.

6

1 ½ in. (1.5 cm) ½ in (1.5cm)

2 Fold the top down and the bottom up.

3 Turn over and fold forward along the dotted lines.

4 Fold in half.

5 Completed case.

1 Crease by folding in half.

2

3

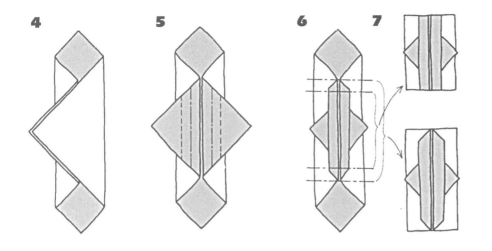

tion of the vertical dotted lines. The horizontal dotted lines at Step 6 indicate possible folding lines that allow you to adjust the size of the case depending on the size of the tissue of other items you may want to place in the case.

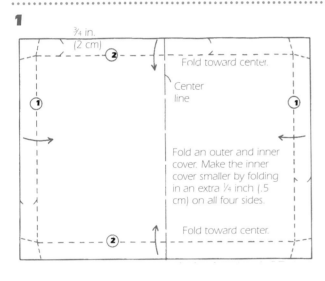

1

¾ in. (2 cm)

Fold toward center.

Center line

Fold an outer and inner cover. Make the inner cover smaller by folding in an extra ¼ inch (.5 cm) on all four sides.

Fold toward center.

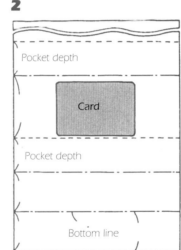

2

Pocket depth

Card

Pocket depth

Bottom line

Fold the bottom up and back along the dotted line as shown in Step 3.

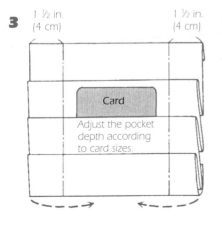

3 1 ½ in. (4 cm)   1 ½ in. (4 cm)

Card

Adjust the pocket depth according to card sizes.

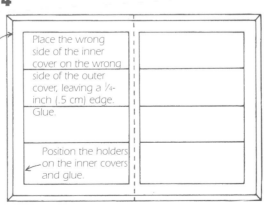

4

Place the wrong side of the inner cover on the wrong side of the outer cover, leaving a ¼-inch (.5 cm) edge. Glue.

Position the holders on the inner covers and glue.

Card Holders and Tissue Holder

Page 41, Projects 1-3

1) Card Holder

In addition to paper you will need: White craft glue

Paper: Two sheets of dark paper (for the inside holder), both size 7 x 18 inches (18 x 45.5 cm). Two sheets of paper for the outer and inner cover, both size 9 ½ x 12 inches (24 x 30.5 cm).

Instructions: Fold the card holders first (Steps 2-3) before making the covers. The depth of the pockets for the card holders will depend on the size of your cards. As you fold, adjust the depth to fit. Make the inner cover smaller, folding it in toward the center an extra ¼ inch (.5 cm) on all four sides.

Tip: Combine printed paper with color-coordinated solid colors for a distinctive look.

2) Business Card Holder

In addition to paper you will need:
White craft glue

Paper: One sheet of printed paper, size 6 ½ x 9 ½ inches (16.5 x 31.5 cm). One sheet solid-color paper size 6½x 12½ inches (16.5 x 31.5 cm.)

Instructions: Fold the patterned paper and solid-color paper separately then glue together. The finished width of the card holder should be approximately 5 inches (24 cm).

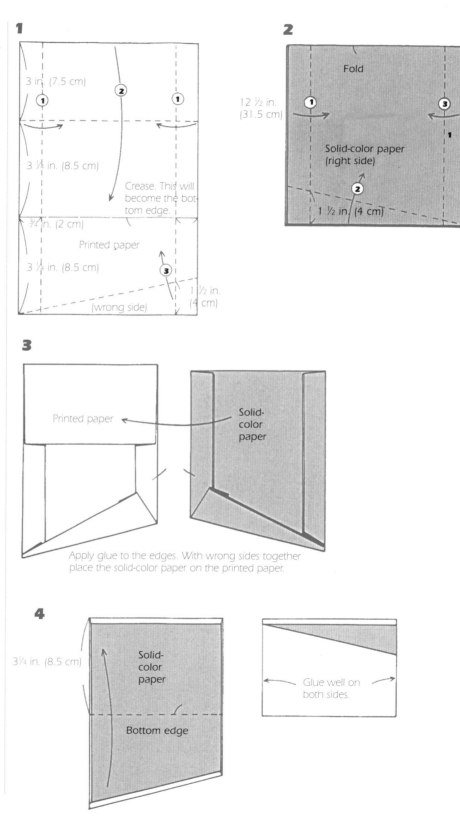

1

3 in. (7.5 cm)

3 ¼ in. (8.5 cm)

Crease. This will become the bottom edge.

¾ in. (2 cm)

Printed paper

3 ¼ in. (8.5 cm)

1 ½ in. (4 cm)

(wrong side)

2

Fold

12 ½ in. (31.5 cm)

Solid-color paper (right side)

1 ½ in. (4 cm)

3

Printed paper

Solid-color paper

Apply glue to the edges. With wrong sides together place the solid-color paper on the printed paper.

4

3¼ in. (8.5 cm)

Solid-color paper

Bottom edge

Glue well on both sides.

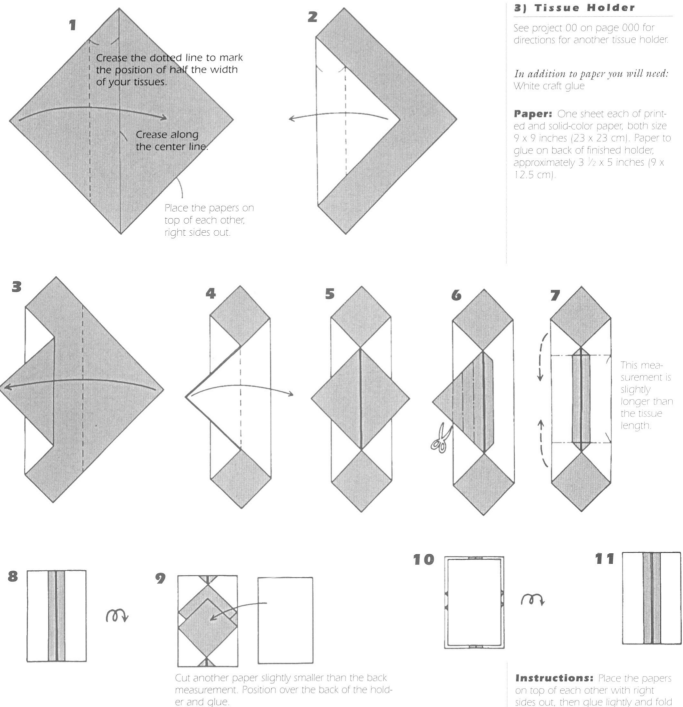

3) Tissue Holder

See project 00 on page 000 for directions for another tissue holder.

In addition to paper you will need: White craft glue

Paper: One sheet each of printed and solid-color paper, both size 9 x 9 inches (23 x 23 cm). Paper to glue on back of finished holder, approximately 3 ½ x 5 inches (9 x 12.5 cm).

1 Crease the dotted line to mark the position of half the width of your tissues.

Crease along the center line.

Place the papers on top of each other, right sides out.

7 This measurement is slightly longer than the tissue length.

9 Cut another paper slightly smaller than the back measurement. Position over the back of the holder and glue.

Instructions: Place the papers on top of each other with right sides out, then glue lightly and fold as one. Adjust the size of the holder to fit the tissues by moving the position of the dotted line in Step 1. Lay the center of the tissues on the center line of the paper to find this position.

Bath Baskets

Page 42, Projects 1-3

1) Trapezoid Box

Paper: Use wrapping paper or wallpaper scraps, size 15 x 15 inches (38 x 38 cm)

Instructions: Begin by making Square Fold B on page 00 then follow Steps 1-7.

Tip: Crease well in each step. Sharp folds will make the container look more solid. At Step 6, you can fold the triangle-shaped flaps underneath or you can tuck them into the sides.

2) Basket with Handle

In addition to paper you will need: White craft glue

Paper: One sheet of printed gift wrap and one sheet of heavyweight plain paper, both size 15 x 15 inches (38 cm x 38 cm),

Instructions: Place the papers on top of each other with right sides facing out, then fold as one. To begin, crease the papers along the dotted lines as shown in Step 1.

Tip: You will need to glue the handle in place.

Begin with Square Fold Box on page 53.

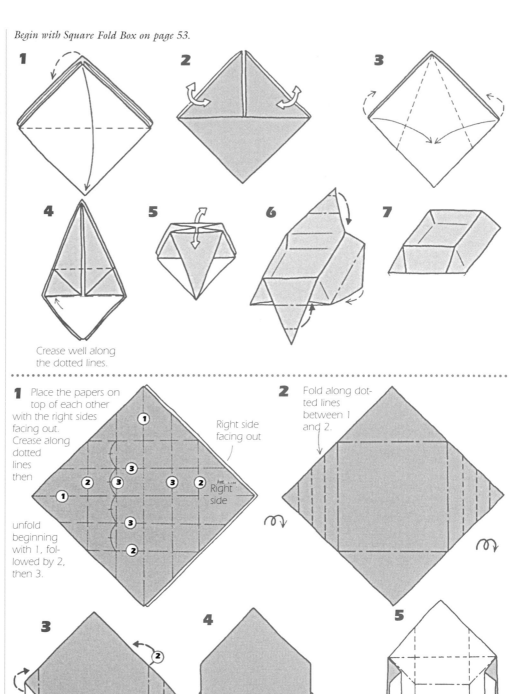

Crease well along the dotted lines.

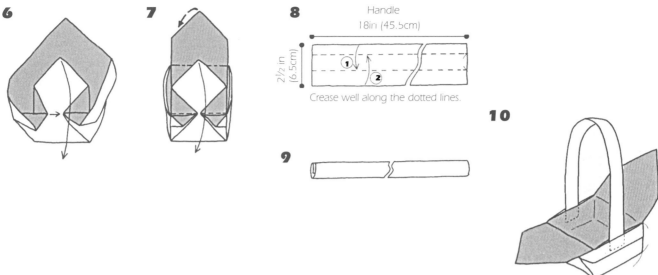

8

Handle
18in (45.5cm)

2½ in (6.5cm)

Crease well along the dotted lines.

Begin with Triangular Fold on page 54.

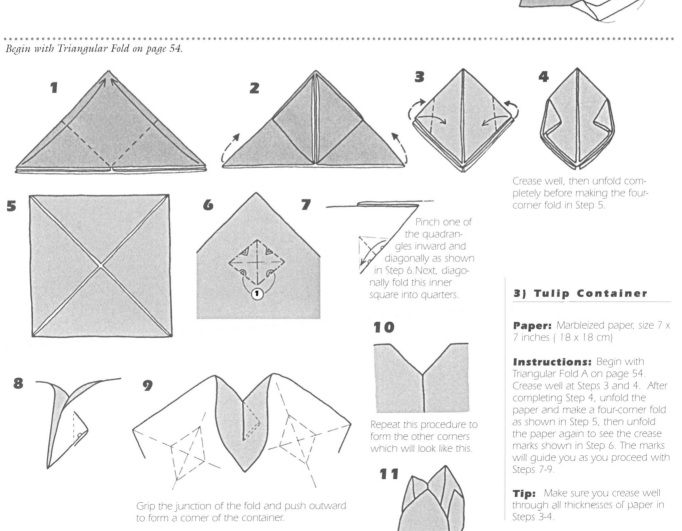

Crease well, then unfold completely before making the four-corner fold in Step 5.

7 Pinch one of the quadrangles inward and diagonally as shown in Step 6.Next, diagonally fold this inner square into quarters.

10 Repeat this procedure to form the other corners which will look like this.

Grip the junction of the fold and push outward to form a corner of the container.

3) Tulip Container

Paper: Marbleized paper, size 7 x 7 inches (18 x 18 cm)

Instructions: Begin with Triangular Fold A on page 54. Crease well at Steps 3 and 4. After completing Step 4, unfold the paper and make a four-corner fold as shown in Step 5, then unfold the paper again to see the crease marks shown in Step 6. The marks will guide you as you proceed with Steps 7-9.

Tip: Make sure you crease well through all thicknesses of paper in Steps 3-4.

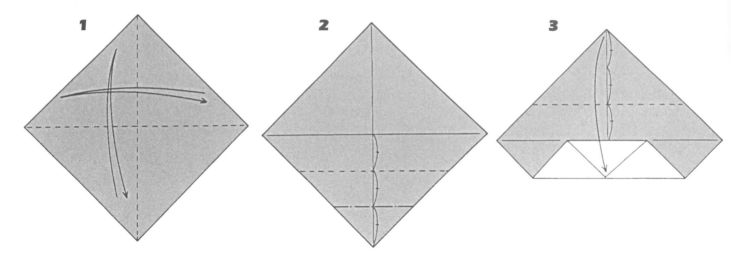

Square Small-Item Containers

Page 43, Projects 1-3

1) Square Container A

In addition to paper you will need: White craft glue

Paper: One sheet each of printed and solid-color paper, both size 6 x 6 inches (15 x 15 cm).

Instructions: Before folding, glue the two sheets of paper together with the right sides out, then fold as one. After you've finished the first side by completing Steps 9-15, work to your right, repeating Steps 10-14 to complete the folds for the next two sides. As you complete the folds for each side, turn the paper clockwise so a square edge is always parallel to your body. After you've completed three sides and get to the last one it will look different since it has no visible corner to fold to the opposite end as in Steps 14 and 15. Open the flap to your left and reverse the lower left-hand corner fold, tucking it under the flap you will be working on. (Be careful to not open the right-side flap). Grasp the point of the triangle and bring it to the opposite edge. From here proceed with steps 10-13 to make fold for the last side.

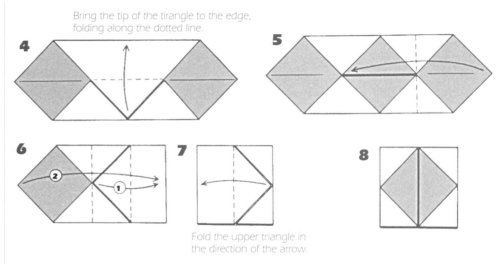

Bring the tip of the triangle to the edge, folding along the dotted line.

Fold the upper triangle in the direction of the arrow.

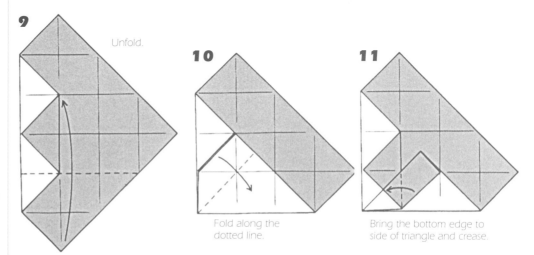

Unfold.

Fold along the dotted line.

Bring the bottom edge to side of triangle and crease.

12

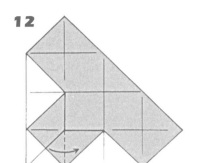

Fold triangle over on dotted line.

13 Open the edge indicated by the arrows while bringing the triangle up and flatten.

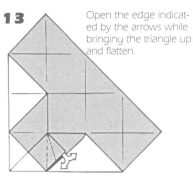

Prepare the paper this way to create the border as shown in the photo for this project on page 43. Trim two sides of the printed paper each ¼ inch (.6 cm). Place the papers on top of each other with right sides facing out so there is a ⅛-inch (.3 cm) "border" of solid-color paper all around. Glue, then fold as one.

14

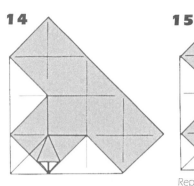

15

Repeat Steps 10-14 on the next two corners. To make the last corner fold, refer to the instructions.

16

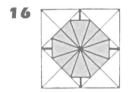

Place the papers together so there is a ⅛-in. (.3 cm) border of solid-color paper showing on all four edges.

Solid-color paper

Printed paper

Complete by following Steps 1-15.

Begin with Steps 1-8 for project 1.

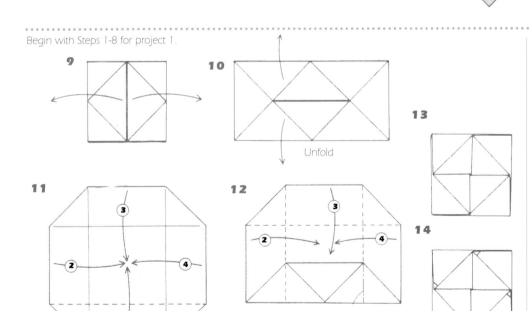

Unfold

Reverse the fold on the bottom right crease, tucking it under the bottom flap.

2) Square Container B

In addition to paper you will need: White craft glue

Paper: One sheet each of printed and solid-color paper, both size 6 x 6 inches (15 x 15 cm).

Instructions: Before folding, glue the two sheets together with right sides out, then fold as one. To begin, follow Steps 1-8 for Square Container A, project 1 on pages 112-113, then proceed with Steps 9-13 for this project. To sharpen the folds, place the finished container under heavy books or a similar weight for a short time.

3) Pinwheel Container

In addition to paper you will need:
White craft glue

Paper: One sheet each of printed and solid-color paper, both size 6 x 6 inches (15 x 15 cm).

Instructions: Before folding, glue the two sheets of paper together with right sides out, then fold as one. To begin, follow Steps 1-8 for Square Container A, project 1 on page 112, then proceed with Steps 9-20 for this project. Steps 10-13 create the crease lines for the folds in Steps 14-20.

Octagonal Containers

Page 44, Projects 1-5

1) Flower A

In addition to paper you will need:
White craft glue

Paper: One sheet each of printed paper and solid-color paper, both size 6 x 6 inches (15 x 15 cm).

Instructions: You can make this project without a border or with a border as shown in the photo on page 44. To make a border, trim the patterned paper 1/4 inch (.6 cm) on two of its sides. Place the papers on top each other with right sides facing out so there is a 1/8 inch (.3 cm) border of solid-color paper all the way around. Glue the papers together, then fold as one. At Step 10, fold the last triangular flap and tuck it in by placing the angular edge made by the first fold on top.

Tip: Make the folds crisp and accurate. The uniformity of design depends on making the angles and triangular flaps the same size as you work around the paper.

Begin with Steps 1-8 for project 1.

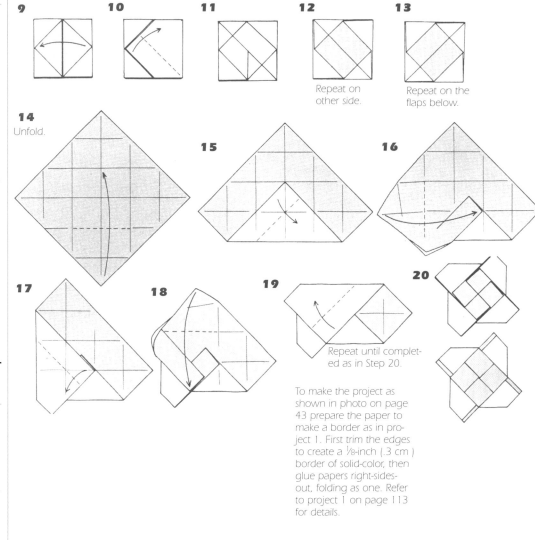

12 Repeat on other side.

13 Repeat on the flaps below.

14 Unfold.

19 Repeat until completed as in Step 20.

To make the project as shown in photo on page 43 prepare the paper to make a border as in project 1. First trim the edges to create a 1/8-inch (.3 cm) border of solid-color, then glue papers right-sides-out, folding as one. Refer to project 1 on page 113 for details.

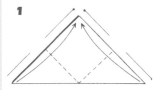

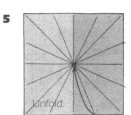

5 Unfold.

6

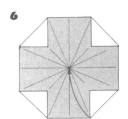

Fold the bottom flaps up so that the stars meet as shown in Step 7.

7

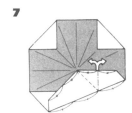

Crease along the dotted lines to make a triangle. Fold the triangle down, making a triangular flap. Working counter clockwise, repeat around the paper as shown in Step 9.

8

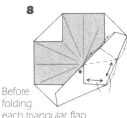

Before folding each triangular flap down, position the paper so the angles beneath it look like this.

9

To fold the last triangular flap, open the paper just enough to make the fold, then place the angular edge made by the first fold on top of it.

10

To make the project as shown in the photo on page 44 prepare the paper with a border as explained in the instructions.

....

(2)

5 Unfold.

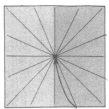

Bring the star to the center and fold.

6

Bring the triangle to the center, making sure that the diagonal crease goes beneath the fold.

7

Crease well. Before folding each triangular flap down, position the paper so the angles beneath it look like this.

8

Continue folding the triangular flaps down, working counter clockwise around the paper as shown.

2) Flower B

Refer to the general instructions for project 1. Follow Steps 1-4 for project 1. Then begin with Steps 5-10 for this project.

9

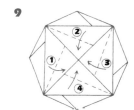

10

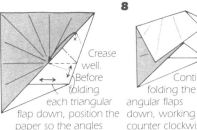

To make the project as shown in the photo on page 44 prepare the paper with a border as explained in the general instructions for project 1.

....

(3) **9**

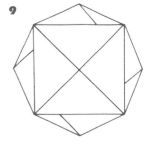 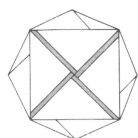

To make the project as shown in the photo on page 44 prepare the paper with a border as explained in the general instructions for project 1.

3) Variation on Flower B, project 2

Refer to the general instructions for project 1. Follow Steps 1-4 for project 1 and Steps 5-8 for project 2 to complete this project as shown.

4) Variation on Flower B, project 2

Refer to the general instructions for project 1. Follow Steps 1-4 for project 1 and Steps 1-8 for project 2 before folding the triangles as shown to complete this project this project.

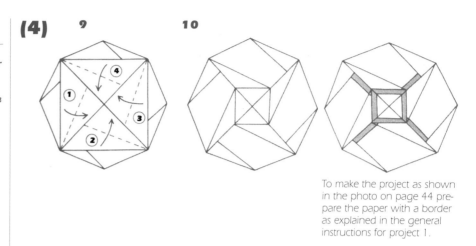

To make the project as shown in the photo on page 44 prepare the paper with a border as explained in the general instructions for project 1.

5) Variation on Flower B, project 2

Refer to the general instructions for project 1. Follow Steps 1-4 for project 1 and Steps 5-8 for project 2 before folding the center in the direction of the arrows as shown to complete this project.

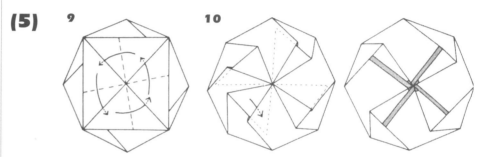

To make the project as shown in the photo on page 44 prepare the paper with a border as explained in the general instructions for project 1.

HOLIDAYS

1

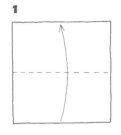

2

3

Open and reverse the folds along the crease lines.

Crease along the dotted lines.

4

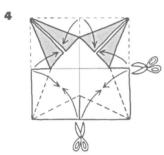

5

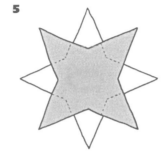

Cut into the ends of the horizontal and vertical center fold lines, making four cuts, then fold as indicated.

Make two stars for each coaster, place on top of each other and glue.

1) Star Coasters

In addition to paper you will need:
Scissors
White craft glue

Paper: Two sheets of metallic-colored paper or shiny paper, size 3 x 3 inches (7.5 x 7.5 cm).

Instructions: For each coaster, make two stars then glue together.

2) Santa Napkins

In addition to paper you will need:
Scissors
White craft glue

Paper: One sheet each of white and pink paper, both size 6 x 6 inches (15 x 15 cm). Small pieces of black, red, and white paper for eyes, mouth, and beard. One red paper napkin.

Instructions: For Step 1, place the white paper on top of the pink paper then fold as one. Glue the eyes, beard, and mouth to the face.

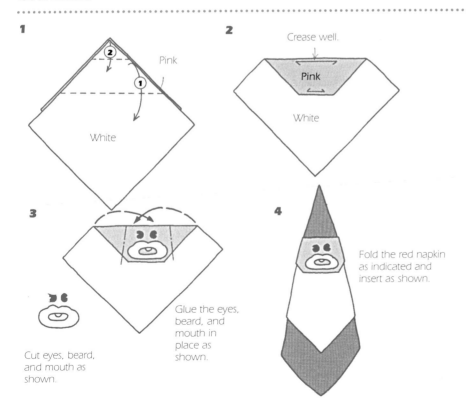

1

Pink

White

2

Crease well.

Pink

White

3

Cut eyes, beard, and mouth as shown.

Glue the eyes, beard, and mouth in place as shown.

4

Fold the red napkin as indicated and insert as shown.

Valentine Envelopes

Page 46, Projects 1-3

1) Solid-Color Envelope with Triangles

In addition to paper, you will need:
Scissors
White craft glue

Paper: One sheet solid-color paper, size 15¾ x 20 1/2 inches (40 x 52 cm). Three sheets solid-color paper for triangles, each size 6 x 6 inches (15 x 15 cm).

Instructions: At Step 4, make the triangles as follows: Cut three triangles out of three separate sheets of paper, making each of them with two sides measuring 5 inches (12.5 cm). Leave one triangle that size. Trim the corresponding two sides of another triangle 1/8 inch (.3 cm) smaller. Glue it on the larger triangle, leaving a 1/8 inch (.3 cm) border showing. Repeat the process to make a third, smaller triangle. To make the small triangle begin with three triangles, each with two sides measuring 2 inches (5cm). Then repeat the process for the larger triangle.

2) Printed Envelope with Triangles

Paper: One sheet solid-color paper, size 9 x 15½ inches (23 x 39.5 cm). One sheet heavyweight printed paper, size 12 x 24 inches (30.5 x 61 cm). Tissue paper cut into a triangle with two sides measuring 6 ½ inches (17 cm). Solid or printed paper cut into a triangle with two sides measuring 5 inches (12.5 cm).

Instructions: If you are using a printed paper with a large pattern, take care when folding so the desired portion of the print will show on the top when finished.

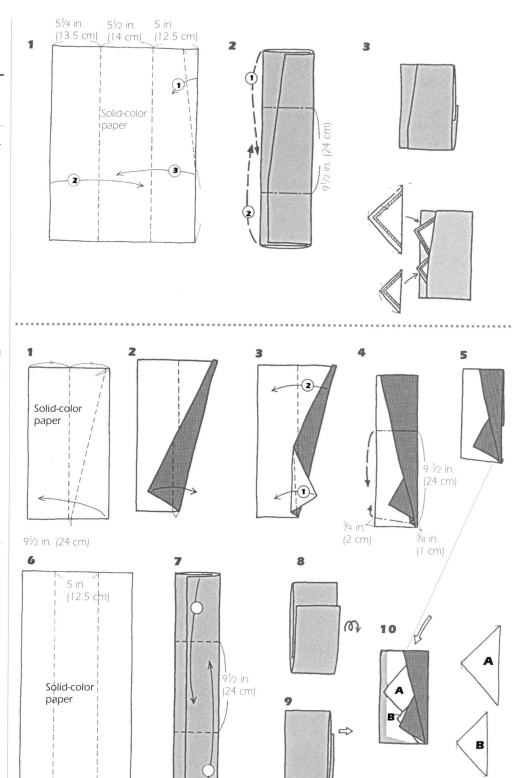

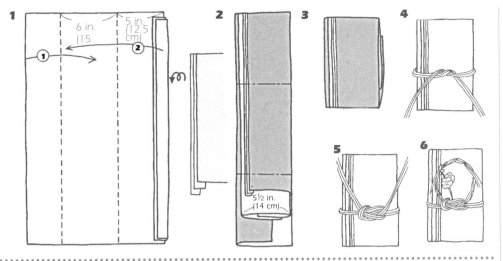

1
6 in. 5 in.
(15 (12.5 cm)

2
5½ in. (14 cm)

3

4

5

6

3) Print Envelope with Tie

Paper: One sheet each of printed and solid-color paper, both size 16 x 20 ½ inches (40.5 x 52 cm). Two sheets of solid-color paper in different colors, both size 1 ¼ x 21 inches (3 x 53.5 cm). Paper strings, five each in two different colors of solid-color paper.

Instructions: If you are using a printed paper with a large pattern, take care when folding so the desired portion of the print will show on the top when finished. Place the two large sheets os paper on top of each other with right sides facing out. Position so the solid-color paper is facing up before beginning Step 1.

Valentine's Day

Pages 47, Projects 1-4

1) Gift Box with Lid and Topless Gift Container

Paper: For the bottom of the gift box with lid use one sheet of solid-color and one sheet of printed heavyweight gift-wrap paper, both size 12 x 10 inches (30.5 x 25.5 cm); for the lid use one sheet each of the same, both size 13 x 11 inches (33.5 x 28 cm). For the topless container, use one sheet each of the same above, size 9 x 10 inches (23 x 25.5 cm).

Instructions: Place the papers on top of each other with the right sides out. At Step 7, open carefully to avoid tearing the papers.

---

1 Bottom
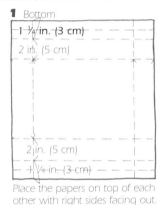
1 ¼ in. (3 cm)
2 in. (5 cm)
2 in. (5 cm)
1 ¼ in. (3 cm)

Place the papers on top of each other with right sides facing out.

2 Lid
1 ¼ in. (3 cm)
2 ¼ in. (5.5 cm)
2 ¼ in. (5.5 cm)
1 ¼ in. (3 cm)

The paper for the lid measures 1 inch (2.5 cm) larger than the paper for the bottom.

3
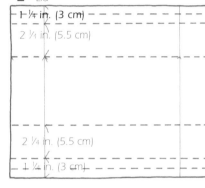
Right side
Wrong side
Turn over.

4
Turn over and repeat on other side.

5
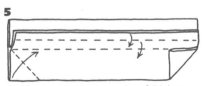
Turn the folded flaps up, then fold the corners into triangles as shown.

6
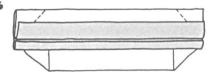
Turn over and repeat on other side.

7
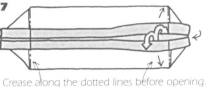
Crease along the dotted lines before opening.

8
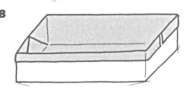

1) Gift Box with Lid and Topless Gift Container (continued)

1 Topless Container

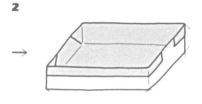

2

→

Follow Steps 3-8 for the gift box above.

From the diagram:
¼ cm (3 cm)
1 ½ in. (3.5 cm)
1 ½ in. (3.5 cm)
¼ cm (3 cm)

2) Hearts

Paper: Solid-color paper in red or pink, size 3 x 11 inches (7.5 x 28 cm) for large; 2 x 8 inches (5 x 20.5 cm) for medium; and 1 ½ x 5½ inches (4 x 14 cm) for small.

Instructions: Bring both edges of the bottom to the center line and fold. At Step 3, fold the top corners to shape the heart.

Tip:
Use metallic-colored or shiny paper for added sparkle.

1

2

3

4

3) Gift Wrapper

In addition to paper you will need:
White Craft Glue

Paper: Gold or silver wrapping paper, size 11 x 11 inches (28 x 28 cm). Contrasting solid-color or printed paper for the bow, size 5 x 2 inches (12.5 x 5 cm).

Instructions: Steps 1-4 show how to fold the bow which you will glue to the wrapper in Step 6.

4) Shirt-Shaped Gift

1

Fold ends along the diagonal dotted lines. At center, fold back along outer vertical lines, then fold forward along inner vertical lines.

2

Crease along the dotted lines. Bring the ends toward the center while opening the triangles.

3

Flatten folded flaps.

4

5

6

Attach bow here.

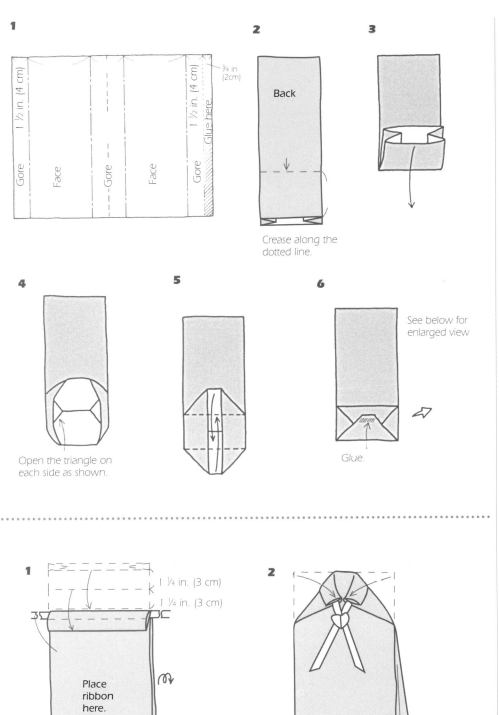

1

Gore · Face · Gore · Face · Gore · Glue here

1 ½ in. (4 cm) · 1 ½ in. (4 cm) · ¾ in (2cm)

2

Back

Crease along the dotted line.

3

4

Open the triangle on each side as shown.

5

6

See below for enlarged view

Glue.

1

1 ¼ in. (3 cm)
1 ¼ in. (3 cm)

Place ribbon here.

2

In addition to paper you will need:
Ribbon, size ½ x 20 inches (1.5 x 51 cm)
White craft glue

Paper: One sheet of printed gift-wrap paper, size 19 x 19 inches (48.5 x 48.5 cm). Pink or red paper for the heart, size 2 ½ x ½ inches (6 x 1.5 cm).

Instructions: After completing Step 6, place the gift in the bag, then proceed with Steps 7-8. Fold a small paper heart as shown in project 2 and glue to the ribbon in step 8.

Holiday Season

Projects 1-8, Page 48

1) Star-Shaped Candy Dishes

In addition to paper you will need:
Scissors

Paper: Two sheets of gold paper, sizes 9 ½ x 9 ½ inches (24 x 24 cm). One sheet each of red and green paper, both size 9 ½ x 9 ½ inches (24 x 24 cm).

Instructions: Begin with the Basic 10-Fold on page 72. As with projects 1-9 on page 72, you will cut the paper once it's folded. Rather than making a curved line as shown for those projects, cut a diagonal line across the paper you've folded (refer to Step 5 of project 3 on page 125). At Step 2 unfold the star, then fanfold to sharpen the creases. This will shape the star, giving it dimension. Make two gold stars, one red, and one green.

2) Bow and Ribbon

In addition to paper you will need:
Scissors
White craft glue
Pinking sheers

Paper: For the bow and ribbon use one sheet each of heavyweight paper in red and green, both size 10 x 26 inches (25.5 x 66 cm). For the cards on the ribbon, use three sheets of heavyweight white paper size 3 x 4 ½ inches (25.5cm x 66cm). For the design motifs, use a variety of holiday-print paper in the sizes given for individual instructions.

Instructions: For the ribbon and bow, begin by cutting 2 ½ inches (6.5 cm)from the bottom width of both the red and green papers, set these aside. Cut the

1

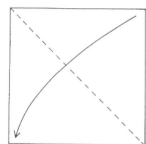

Unfold, then fanfold.

3

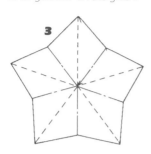

Place one gold star right side up on top of the red star and the other gold star on the green.

A

Use for bow.

Glue red to green. Overlap 2 inches (5 cm) and glue.

B

Make a triangular ribbon-cut on one end and use for ribbon.

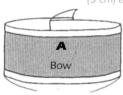

A
Bow

Fanfold A in the center, then circle with C, overlapping C at back to glue.

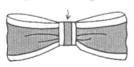

C

Trim the 2 ½ inch (6.5 cm) wide piece of red and green to 7 inches (18 cm) long.

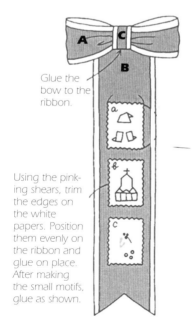

A   C
B

Glue the bow to the ribbon.

Using the pinking shears, trim the edges on the white papers. Position them evenly on the ribbon and glue on place. After making the small motifs, glue as shown.

Hat

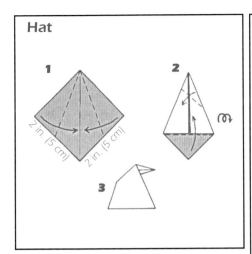

1

2 in. (5 cm)

2 in. (5 cm)

2

3

Holly

Make two.

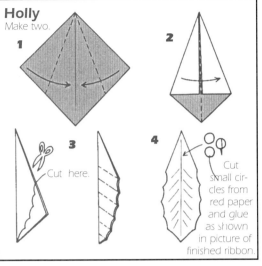

1

2

3

Cut here.

4

Cut small circles from red paper and glue as shown in picture of finished ribbon.

large sheets of red and green papers in half lengthwise. From one of the long edges on each piece of red paper, cut 1 inch (2.5 cm). Glue the red papers on the green, leaving a ½-inch (1.5 cm) border of green showing. One sheet will be for the bow (A) and one for the ribbon (B). From the 2 ½-inch (6.5 cm) wide pieces of red and green cut from the bottom, trim one of the long sides of the red paper 1 inch (2.5 cm). Glue the red paper on the green, leaving a ½-inch (1.5 cm) border of green showing. Use this for C.

Church

Use two sheets of paper with different prints. Place them on each other with right sides out. Begin with Triangular Fold B on page 54.

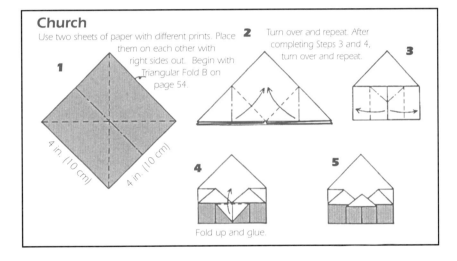

1

4 in. (10 cm)

4 in. (10 cm)

2 Turn over and repeat. After completing Steps 3 and 4, turn over and repeat.

3

4 Fold up and glue.

5

Boots

Make two.

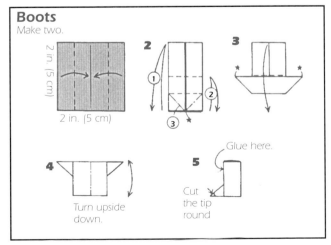

2 in. (5 cm)

2 in. (5 cm)

2

3

4 Turn upside down.

5 Cut the tip round

Glue here.

3) Star

In addition to paper you will need:
Scissors

Paper: Gold and silver papers, size 5 x 5 inches (12.5 x 12.5 cm).

Instructions: Begin with Basic 10-Fold on page 72. As with projects 1-9 on page 72, you will cut the paper once it's folded. Rather than making a curved line as shown for those projects, cut a slanted line diagonally across the paper you've folded as shown in Step 5. Steps 1-4 shows an alternative method for the 10-Fold for those with more experience. If you are unfamiliar with this fold, use the basic instructions on page 72.

4) Stocking and Boot

In addition to paper you will need:
White craft glue
Stapler

Paper: Heavyweight holiday-print silver or gold foil paper, size 14 x 19 inches (35.5 x 48.5 cm) for the longer stocking; size 12 ½ x 14 inches (31.5 x 35.5 cm) for the shorter boot . Heavyweight holiday-print red foil, size 5 x 14 inches (12.5 x 35.5 cm) for the cuff.

Instructions: At Step 1, glue the strip for the cuff to the wrong side of the gold or silver foil. Measure ½ inch (1.5 cm) from the top of the glued cuff and fold back. Then measure 1 ½ inches (5 cm) from the top of that fold and fold back again. At Step 3, crease well along all lines. After you've stapled or glued the overlap in Step 4, shape the boot by tucking the ankle crease into itself, overlapping as necessary with the paper above the crease. For the boot, keep the toe squared; for the stocking, bring the paper that's tucked under the toe out to form a point as shown in the photo on page 48.

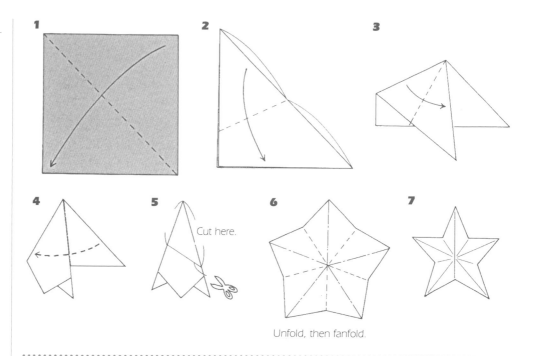

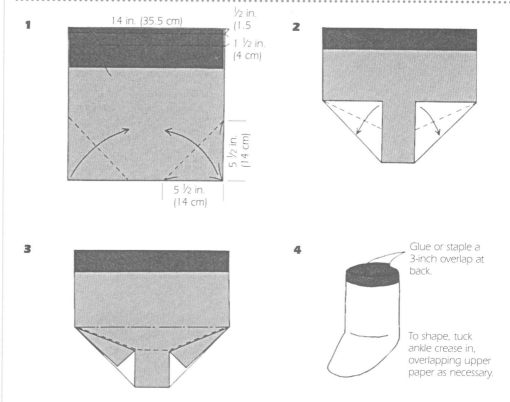

(5)

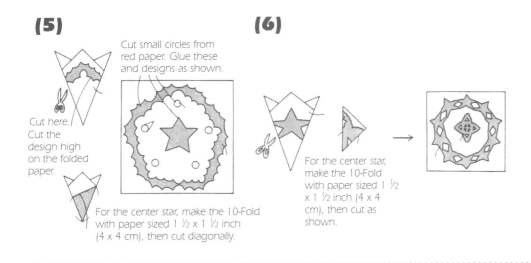

Cut here.
Cut the design high on the folded paper.

Cut small circles from red paper. Glue these and designs as shown.

For the center star, make the 10-Fold with paper sized 1 ½ x 1 ½ inch (4 x 4 cm), then cut diagonally.

(6)

For the center star, make the 10-Fold with paper sized 1 ½ x 1 ½ inch (4 x 4 cm), then cut as shown.

(7)

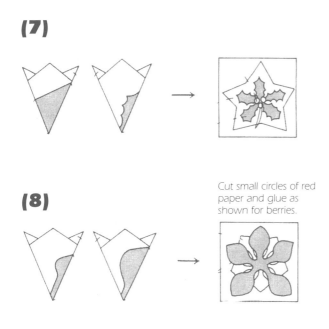

(8)

Cut small circles of red paper and glue as shown for berries.

5-8) Coasters or Cards

In addition to paper you will need:
Scissors
White craft glue

Paper: in holiday colors, size 3 x 3 inches (7.5 x 7.5 cm).

Instructions: For each design, cut the motifs separately, then arrange them on another sheet of 3 x 3-inch (7.5 x 7.5 cm) paper to complete. For each motif, begin with the Basic 10-Fold on page 72. As with projects 1-9 on page 72, you will cut the paper once it's folded.

Tip: Use these for cards or coasters. Try srringing several together to make a garland for decorating a door or window frame. Use metallic-colored papers for extra sparkle.

Wreath Greeting Card

Page 49

In addition to paper you will need:

Scissors
White craft glue

Paper: Use metallic-colored paper for the wreath, regular paper for the card. For the wreath, eight each of gold and green, size 1 ¼ x 1 ¼ inch (3 x 3 cm); for the candle and flame, one each of silver and red, size 1 ½ x 1 ½ inch (4 x 4 cm); for the bow, one each of red and gold, size 1 ½ x 1 ½ inch (4 x 4 cm). For the card, one each of heavyweight red and white paper, both size 5 ½ x 7 inches (14 x 18 cm).

Instructions: Fold as one: gold and green; silver and red; gold and red. To hold the wreath together, place a small amount of glue at the insertion points. For the card, cut the white paper ¼ inch (.5 cm) smaller than the red paper, place it on top of the red paper and glue before folding.

Tip: Since the wreath uses small pieces of paper, you may want to try practicing with larger-size paper first.

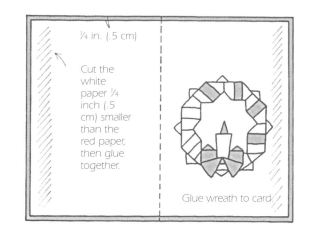

¼ in. (.5 cm)

Cut the white paper ¼ inch (.5 cm) smaller than the red paper, then glue together.

Glue wreath to card.

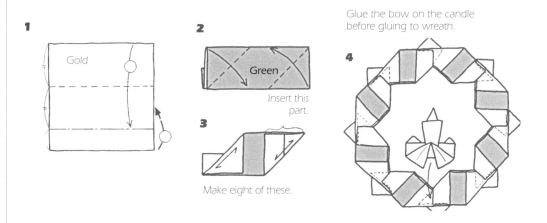

1 Gold

2 Green

Insert this part.

3 Make eight of these.

4 Glue the bow on the candle before gluing to wreath.

Candle

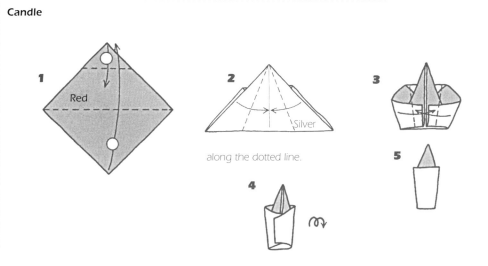

1 Red

2 Silver

along the dotted line.

3

4

5

Bow

1

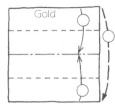

2

3

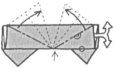

Crease along the dotted lines.
Reverse the rear creases, open
the folds and flatten.

4

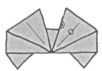

Fanfold

5

Related titles from Lark Books

The Art and Craft of Papermaking
Step-by-Step Instructions for Creating Distinctive Handmade Paper
By Sophie Dawson
$18.95 Paperback ($26.95 Can.), 144 pages, 400 color photos
ISBN 1-887374-24-8
Distributed By Random House

Cover to Cover
Creative Techniques for Making Beautiful Books, Journals & Albums
By Shereen LaPlantz
$16.95 Paperback ($23.95 Can.), 144 pages, 130 color photos, 300 b/w illustrations
ISBN 0-937274-87-9
Distributed by Sterling Publishing

Making Books that Fly, Fold, Wrap, Hide, Pop Up, Twist, and Turn
Books for Kids to Make
By Gwen Diehn
$19.95 Hardback ($27.95 Can.), 96 pages, all color
ISBN 1-887374-023-2
Distributed by Random House

Mexican Papercutting
Simple Techinques for Creating Colorful Cut-Paper Projects
By Kathleen Trenchard
$14.95 Paperback ($20.95 Can.), 96 pages, 70 color photos, 35 b&w photos
ISBN 1-57990-011-9
Distributed by Random House

Scherenschnitte
Designs and Techniques for Traditional Papercutting
By Susanne Schläpfer-Geiser
$18.95 Hardback ($26.95 Can.), 144 pages, 15 color plates, 219 b&w photos & illus.
ISBN 1-887374-18-3
Distributed by Sterling Publishing

The Contemporary Craft of Paper Mache
Techniques, Projects, Inspirations
By Helga Meyer
$29.95 Paperback ($41.95 Can.), 208 pages, 150 color plates, 109 b&w illus.
ISBN 1-887374-11-6
Distributed by Random House

Sources for Origami Supplies

Assorted papers and materials for origami projects are usually available at local bookstores, art and craft supply centers, and gift shops. The following list of mail-order companies represents only a few of the many businesses across the country which offer beautiful and unusual papers.

Aiko's Art Materials Import
3347 N. Clark St.
Chicago, IL 60657
(312) 404-5600
Japanese handmade papers

Back Street Designs
P.O. Box 1213
Athens, AL 35611
assorted papers

Daniel Smith, Inc.
4150 1st Avenue S
P.O. Box 84268
Seattle, WA 98124
(800) 426-6740
assorted papers and art supplies

Fascinating Folds
http://www.fascinating-folds.com/
P.O. Box 10070
Glendale, AZ 85318
(800) 968-2418
origami and other papers

Kim's Crane Origami Supplies & Crafts
http://www.kimscrane.com/
3106 Hannah's Pond Lane
Herndon, VA 20171-2253
(703) 758-0373
e-mail: kcrane@kimscrane.com
origami papers

Pearl Paint
http://www.pearlpaint.com
308 Canal Street
New York City, NY 10013
(800) 221-6845
assorted papers and art supplies

Sax Arts & Crafts
P.O. Box 510710
New Berlin, WI 53151
(414) 784-6880
assorted papers and art supplies